Doing a great work

Doing a great work

Ezra and Nehemiah simply explained

Stan K. Evers

 EVANGELICAL PRESS

EVANGELICAL PRESS
12 Wooler Street, Darlington, Co. Durham, DL1 1RQ, England

© Evangelical Press 1996
First published 1996

British Library Cataloguing in Publication Data available

ISBN 0 85234 346 9

Printed and bound in Great Britain at the Bath Press, Avon.

In fond memory of my parents:
Stanley William Evers (1915-1980)
Peggy Primrose Evers (1919-1990)

Contents

Maps

Preface

Writing this commentary began with a series of Bible studies on Ezra which ran from September 1989 until March 1990. I turned to various commentaries for help, only to discover that many of these were either very scholarly, with little application, or too devotional and lacking in serious exposition. Then I had an idea: why not write a commentary on Ezra containing exposition of, and application arising from, the biblical text — a commentary to inform the mind and to move the heart? Later it occurred to me that Ezra would be incomplete without Nehemiah. Ezra and Nehemiah have become like old friends.

Some time ago a friend reminded me that it took only fifty-two days for Nehemiah to build Jerusalem's wall; he wanted to know why it was taking me so long to write my book! Here it is at last!

I am indebted to previous writers on Ezra and Nehemiah, but especially to Derek Kidner, whose *Tyndale Commentary* has helped me to understand these two books. The plan of the gates of Jerusalem is taken from Kidner and the map of the exiles' journey from Persia to Judah is based on the *American Life Application Bible* (Tyndale House Publishers, 1993).

Special thanks to my wife, Maureen, to the members of Potton Baptist Church and to the editorial staff of Evangelical Press, who have encouraged me to write this book.

Stan K. Evers

Ezra

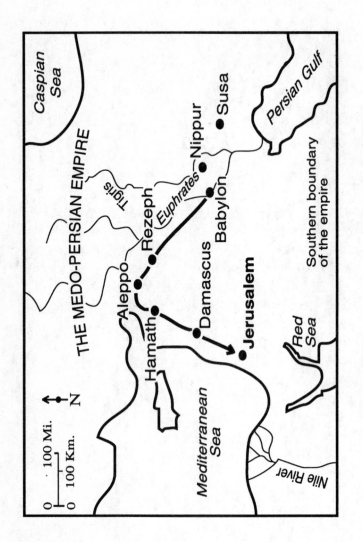

Map 1. The exiles' journey from Persia to Judah

1.
Introducing Ezra

Why should Christians read the books of two obscure Jewish leaders who lived over four hundred years before Jesus Christ? We live in a modern world, so what is the point of reading these antiquarian documents? The paramount reason why we ought to read any portion of the Bible is that 'All Scripture is God-breathed and is useful ...' (2 Tim. 3:16). It seems to me that both the books of Ezra and Nehemiah have a special useful-ness for evangelicals at the present time.

In an age of experienced-centred, clap-happy worship and entertainment-orientated evangelism the books of Ezra and Nehemiah direct our thoughts to a holy God who demands reverent worship and uncompromising loyalty from his people. Furthermore, these two writers call us back to a renewed obedience to God's Word, a fresh realization of the power of prayer and wholehearted commitment to the work of God in fellowship with the people of God.

So then let me introduce you to Ezra...

The story so far

The books of Ezra and Nehemiah continue the story of God's people from the books of the Chronicles. The last two verses of 2 Chronicles are quoted almost word for word in the opening verses of Ezra. The two books of Chronicles record the death of Saul, trace the reigns of David and Solomon until the time of the division of the nation in 937 B.C., then relate events in the northern kingdom of Israel and the southern kingdom of Judah. Israel was taken captive by the Assyrians in 722 B.C. but most of the Israelites never returned home.

The continuing story

In spite of warnings from the prophets, such as Jeremiah and Isaiah, and the defeat of Israel by the Assyrians nearly twenty years before, the Judeans continued in their persistent disobedience of God. Therefore God allowed Nebuchadnezzar to march into Judah in 586 B.C. Jerusalem was captured and destroyed, Zedekiah the king was blinded and taken into Babylon and many of the Jews were deported with him (2 Kings 24:18 - 25:30; 2 Chron. 36:11-21).

The return home

Ezra opens with some Jews returning home to Judah in 537 B.C.: 'Chapters 1-6 tell the story of those next twenty years when, led by Zerubbabel, they faced much discouragement, but eventually finished rebuilding the Temple. Ezra himself is not introduced until 7:1. He led another group of exiles home in about 458 B.C. Chapters 7-10 tell of the way in which he rebuilt the people themselves into a people whose lives were pleasing to God.'[1] The book of Ezra covers about eighty years.

Why did the Jews travel back to Judah? The historical events recorded in the books of Ezra and Nehemiah were all part of God's plan to preserve a pure people for the setting up of Christ's kingdom. Israel must continue as a distinct and holy nation so that the promises relating to the coming of the Messiah would be fulfilled. The advent of the Saviour hinged on the faithfulness of the people of God. The church is now God's 'holy nation' whose godly conduct prepares them for, and speeds the coming of, 'the day of God' (1 Peter 2:9; 2 Peter 3:11-13).

The helper

Ezra is a shortened form of the Hebrew name Azariah, which means, 'The Lord has helped.' God, who helped Ezra, used his servant as a helper of his people. Ezra was a priest and scholar who became 'Secretary of State for Jewish affairs under Artaxerxes'.[2] His book, which was written in Hebrew and Aramaic (Ezra 4:8 - 6:18; 7:12-26 are the Aramaic sections), is partly his own memoir (Ezra 7:27 - 9:15 is in the first person) and partly comprised of official Persian documents (e.g. Ezra 6:1-12). However, it is interesting to note that the book of Ezra is never quoted in the New Testament. Does this detract from its value? No, because it is a portion of the Scripture given by God which is 'useful for teaching, rebuking, correcting and training in righteousness' (2 Tim. 3:16).

At the end of the book Ezra (the priest and scribe) disappears from the record until thirteen years later and Nehemiah moves onto the centre of the stage. Ezra continued to labour among the people of God but he was not the prominent figure. Nehemiah arrived in Jerusalem, with a further batch of exiles, thirteen years after Ezra in 445 B.C. The book of Ezra relates how the temple was rebuilt, whereas Nehemiah tells us how the city of Jerusalem was reconstructed. These two books cover 'a little over a hundred years, from the year 538 B.C. when Cyrus sent the exiles home to re-erect their temple to

some point around 430, or in the decade when Nehemiah
exercised his second term of office in Jerusalem.'[3] In the
Hebrew Bible Ezra and Nehemiah are one book. A Latin
translation of the Bible known as the Vulgate was the first
edition of the Bible to separate Ezra and Nehemiah into two
books.

There is an ongoing debate among biblical scholars concerning the order of Ezra and Nehemiah. Some have suggested
that Nehemiah came to Jerusalem in 444 B.C. and that Ezra
followed him forty-six years later, in 398 B.C. These theories
cannot be true because we are told quite clearly that Ezra
'came up to Jerusalem in the seventh year of King Artaxerxes',
i.e., 458 B.C. (Ezra 7:7) and that Nehemiah arrived on the
scene 'in the twentieth year' of the same king, i.e., 445 B.C.
(Neh. 1:1; 2:1).

To gain a comprehensive view of the 'Restoration Era' you
need to read the books of Ezra, Nehemiah, Haggai, Zechariah
and Malachi, while a glimpse into affairs in Persia during the
same period is given in the book of Esther.[4] You may like to
keep a bookmark in the chronological chart at the end of the
book!

2.
Home at last!

Please read Ezra chapter 1

Imagine living in a strange land, far away from home, where a different language is spoken and you have to build a new life. Think of all the problems that would cause you. Then one day you are given permission to return to your native land. This was the experience of the Jews who were compelled to live for seventy years in the land of Babylon (now in Iraq) and then in 538 B.C. were allowed to travel home. The journey to Judah was the outcome of a decree issued by the Persian king, Cyrus, but behind this edict was the plan of the sovereign God, who was preparing the Jewish race for the coming of Christ, the Saviour of the world.

The proclamation of Cyrus (1:1-4)

The opening verse roots the proclamation in the **'first year of Cyrus'**. Secular history records that 'the first year of Cyrus' began officially in the Jewish month of Nisan (March-April) 538 B.C. This Cyrus was actually Cyrus II, also known as Cyrus the Great, the fourth in a line of kings of Anzan, in Susiana, known to the Hebrews as Elam. Cyrus, who was the son of Cambyses I and grandson of Cyrus I, united the Persians, defeated the Medes (Media is now in north-west Iran) and conquered the Babylonians in October 539 B.C.

Cyrus eventually ruled over a large empire stretching from the Aegean Sea (between Greece and Turkey) to India. He died nine years later fighting the Massegetai tribes east of the Caspian Sea in the summer of 530 B.C. His body was returned to the Persian capital, Pasargadae, for burial. Cyrus was succeeded by his son Cambyses (530-522 B.C.). The Persians were finally routed by Alexander the Great, King of Macedonia (356-323 B.C.). It was God who brought this powerful monarch, Cyrus, to pre-eminence for the deliverance of the Jews. The preservation of the Jews was vital for the fulfilment of the Messianic prophecies.

In the British Museum there is a clay barrel found in Babylon, known as the Cyrus Cylinder, which recounts the victories of Cyrus the Great and his policy of permitting his citizens to return to their various homelands. This astute policy of Cyrus created peace and contentment among the races under Persian jurisdiction. This cylinder confirms that Cyrus gave the Jews permission to go home and rebuild their temple. The proclamation of Cyrus may have been written in Aramaic, the language of diplomacy in the Persian empire.

Ezra tells us that the decree of Cyrus the Persian was passed **'in order to fulfil the word of the Lord spoken by Jeremiah'** (1:1). Some two hundred years before the release of the captive Jews the prophet Jeremiah had set the time limit of the exile as seventy years: 'This is what the Lord says: "When the seventy years are completed for Babylon, I will come to you and fulfil my gracious promise to bring you back to this place"' (Jer. 29:10). Ezra does not refer to the prediction of Isaiah in which God actually named Cyrus as the deliverer of his people: 'Cyrus ... is my shepherd and will accomplish all that I please' (Isa. 44:28).

Josephus, the Jewish historian, states that Cyrus was shown these prophecies and was 'seized by a strong desire and ambition to do what had been written'.[1] If Josephus' account is accurate, how did Cyrus the Persian know about the words of a Jewish prophet? Perhaps it was Daniel who directed his attention to the words of Jeremiah. Daniel, who was taken captive by Nebuchadnezzar, rose to a high position in the court of Babylon some seventy years before Cyrus came to power. He served therefore under Nebuchadnezzar, Belshazzar, Darius and Cyrus, from 605 B.C. until about 536 B.C., the third year of the reign of Cyrus (Dan. 1:1-5; 10:1). Jeremiah's ministry began before the exile and continued among the remnant in Judah after the majority had been taken to Babylon. Daniel and Jeremiah were therefore contemporaries. It was God who had placed Daniel in just the right place to forward his divine decrees.

An intriguing question arises from the quotation of Jeremiah's prophecy: when did the seventy years actually begin and finish? The answer is not as simple as it might seem. If we take the exile as the starting-point, only forty-eight years elapsed between the fall of Jerusalem and the decree of Cyrus, not seventy. Some count the years from the demolition of the temple in 586 B.C. to its completion in 515 B.C. 'on the third day of the month Adar, in the sixth year of the reign of King Darius' (Ezra 6:15). According to Jewish reckoning the sixth year of Darius would have extended from Nisan (April/May) 516 to Adar (February-March) 515 B.C. The solution is probably to interpret Jeremiah's prophecy as relating to Babylonian domination, counted either from the fall of Nineveh, 612 B.C., or Nebuchadnezzar's ascension, 605 B.C., to the overthrow of the Babylonians in 539 B.C. — a period of approximately seventy years and therefore a remarkably exact prophecy.[2] Whatever the precise dating of the seventy years, the important point to emphasize is that 'When God makes a promise, no matter how long it takes, he always keeps his word.'[3]

Another question suggests itself: why did a pagan king issue an edict which favoured God's people? Verse 1 supplies the answer from the divine viewpoint: **'The Lord moved the**

heart of Cyrus king of Persia.' God himself implanted the idea in the mind of the monarch and gave him the ability to translate that idea into motion. Whatever political motives lay behind Cyrus' decree, God was working out his own plans. God had not forgotten his exiled people in Babylon; therefore he aroused the heart of Cyrus to release the Jews. The Lord does not abandon his people when they suffer and face temptation. He is sovereign and can bring good out of all their painful experiences. Read again Romans 8:28! The God who motivated Cyrus to fulfil his designs is powerful to answer the prayers of his people for comfort and strength. He is in control of the greatest nations and rulers even today. His purposes are not hindered by wicked men; he governs the whole of history for the benefit of his church.

There is no evidence that Cyrus knew God in a saving way even though he favoured the people of God. It is fascinating to discover how much he knew about God. He acknowledges his goodness, **'The Lord ... has given me'**, and his greatness, **'The Lord, the God of heaven...'** (1:2). He bows to the supreme King who has the authority to instruct him to build a temple for the Jews at Jerusalem (1:2-3). He had grasped so much about God, yet he was not a child of God. Verse 2 reminds us that head-knowledge of God and usefulness to God do not necessarily guarantee conversion to God. Balaam (Num. 22-24) and Judas Iscariot are other biblical examples of men who knew about God and were used by God, but neither were converted men. The same will be true of some on the Day of Judgement (Matt. 7:22-23).

The preparation of the Jews (1:5-11)

The migration from Babylon was like the Exodus all over again. Two hundred years earlier Isaiah had spoken of the deliverance from Babylon in language drawn from the time when God used Moses to deliver the Hebrews from Egypt (Isa. 43:14-21; 48:20-21). At the Exodus all the nation went back to the promised land; this time round only a small remnant returned under the leadership of Zerubbabel. It may be that Cyrus was assisted by some of the Jews in drawing up his proclamation, which would explain the undertones of the Exodus motif.

The exiled Jews prayed for years for deliverance as they sang their dirge: 'How can we sing the songs of the Lord while in a foreign land?' (Ps. 137:4), but when at last the opportunity to leave was presented to them the majority refused to turn their back on the land of Babylon. How can we account for the reluctance of God's covenant people to return to the land of promise? We must remember that it was many years since they had left their homeland. Meanwhile they had prospered materially, gaining possessions they were loath to abandon. Others no doubt feared the risks involved in a journey of almost a thousand miles to a land that they had not personally known, where they would have to start a pioneer work of building a desolate country. For them it would be like a child born in England of West Indian parents facing the daunting prospect of going to live in Jamaica. The Jews valued material comforts more than their spiritual heritage. They put their own ease before the Lord's work. The Christian in this materialistic society constantly faces the same temptation today. For example, should a Christian leave a thriving evangelical church which has good expository preaching, and move to an area miles away from a church because he is offered a job with an increased salary? Is it wise for a Christian to frequently work overtime so that he rarely attends the midweek meeting of his church? What should the Christian do who is employed by the DIY store which trades on Sundays? These are some of the problems which can be forced upon Christians in these days.

However, 49,897 of the Jews resolved to trek back to the land of Judah (2:64-65), led by **'the family heads of Judah and Benjamin'** (1:5), the two tribes taken into captivity by the Babylonians. These migrating Jews, like Cyrus, were moved by God **'to go up and build'** (1:5). The population of Israel was small compared with the nation of Israel prior to the exile. 'Now the Lord, as though to emphasize that he is not the God of the big battalions, stirred only a remnant of this remnant into action.'⁴ Whatever God's people accomplished in Judah would not be by their own might or power but through God's power alone (Zech. 4:6). God's people can have no spiritual aspirations nor can engage in any Christian service unless God implants the desire within their hearts and gives them his aid. But God will not do the work for us. We, like the exiles, must get up and go! The life of the believer is a mixture of divine power and human activity. God commands obedience and then assists us to obey.

Were the **'neighbours'** who gave the exiles going-away presents (1:6) the same group as the **'survivors'** (Jews remaining in Babylon) who gave **'freewill offerings for the temple of God in Jerusalem'**? (1:4). I would suggest that the 'neighbours' may have included non-Jews because Cyrus, a non-Jewish sovereign, supervised this distribution and took the lead by restoring the vessels taken by Nebuchadnezzar from the temple (1:7-11). Verse 6 forms another link with the Exodus story and is reminiscent of Exodus 12:35-36, where we read, 'The Israelites did as Moses instructed and asked the Egyptians for articles of silver and gold and for clothing. The Lord had made the Egyptians favourably disposed towards the people, and they gave them what they asked for; so they plundered the Egyptians.' The godliness of the exiles won the respect of their Babylonian neighbours; hence their generosity to the people of God.

We read that the vessels stolen by Nebuchadnezzar (2 Chron. 36:7,9-10) and restored by Cyrus (1:7-11) were desecrated by

King Belshazzar in his drunken revelries (Dan. 5:1-4). Nebuchadnezzar had placed these vessels **'in the temple of his god'** (1:7) to thank his god for victory and to mock the Jews' God, who was too weak to save them. Since God was so careful that none of the utensils should be left behind in Babylon, may we not rest assured that he will take good care of his own dear children for whom the Saviour died? Every believer is more precious in God's sight than the most costly vessels of his temple. Paul compares Christians to vessels in 2 Timothy 2:19-21. The assurance of the believer is grounded in the fact that 'The Lord knows those who are his.' Those who belong to him are vessels of 'gold and silver' who reflect his glory, but those who are not his are vessels of mere 'wood and clay', who bring shame and reproach on the Saviour's lovely name. They appear to be his, but their conduct contradicts their claims. The way to honour him is by holy living.

When all the utensils are catalogued the various pieces add up to 2,499 (1:9-10), yet the total given in verse 11 is 5,400. Is there a contradiction? It seems that the figure in verse 11 must include many small items which were not numbered individually but are included in the grand total. Why does the Holy Spirit guide Ezra to record all these minute details? It may be that we are taught that it is not unspiritual to be organized and disciplined in our Christian lives. Very little is accomplished by shoddy and careless work. Surely the Lord of glory is worthy of our best service!

Another problem concerns the identity of 'Sheshbazzar' in verses 8 and 11. He is probably the same person as Zerubbabel, the governor of Judah. 'In support of this view is the fact that Zerubbabel is said to have laid the foundation of the Temple (Ezra 3:8; 5:2; Zech. 4:9), but in an official letter to Darius, Sheshbazzar is said to have done this (Ezra 5:16).'[5] The foundation may, of course, have been laid by both Zerubbabel and Sheshbazzar! If, on the other hand, the two names refer to the same person then Sheshbazzar was his Persian name and

Zerubbabel his Jewish name. Zerubbabel means 'stranger in Babylon' and Sheshbazzar means 'joy in affliction'. Zerubbabel was the godly grandson of the wicked King Jehoiachin who was taken captive by Nebuchadnezzar (1 Chron. 3:17-19; 2 Kings 24:8-16). Grace does not run in families. It is the gift of God, given to whom he chooses to give it (Rom. 9.15).

Believers who come from Christian homes must not assume that they are in God's family by virtue of their natural birth. Christians who come from ungodly families are not to despair of salvation and usefulness. The same God who chose Zerubbabel can select and use anyone! Salvation is through Jesus Christ alone, but those who are saved by grace are to exhibit that grace in their lives.

When we read the word **'exiles'** (1:11) this does not refer to all the exiles, but only to those who returned to the land of Judah. Physical attachment to the people of God then and worship with his people now do not guarantee divine favour. The return was the fulfilment of prophecy and an act of obedience. Obedience is the hallmark of the true child of God in every age. It is evident as we read the opening chapters of Ezra that Cyrus' directive did not give political freedom to the Jews, but it did give them permission to go up to Jerusalem to rebuild the temple and to renew the worship of God.

3.
Only a list of names?

Please read Ezra chapter 2

Be honest! Did you really read every word of Ezra chapter 2? You were probably tempted to skip it and go on to chapter 3. So was I when writing this book! Though Ezra 2 is a difficult chapter to read it contains some valuable spiritual lessons. The same list with a few variations appears in Nehemiah 7:6-69. These genealogical sections prove that the returning exiles were the legitimate descendants of the Jews who occupied Israel prior to their deportation to Persia. The gift of the land and the preservation of Israel as a distinct nation were tied in with God's plan to send his Son, the Lord Jesus Christ, to earth as the Saviour of the world.

Before we come to the relevance of Ezra 2 to our own lives we ought to survey the various categories mentioned by the scribe. The chapter opens with information about the Jewish leaders (2:1-2), including **'Jeshua'**, or 'Joshua', the high priest of whom we read in Zechariah 3. The **'Nehemiah'** in verse 2 must not, of course, be confused with the cupbearer of Artaxerxes, who lived some eighty years later and wrote the book that bears his name. Likewise **'Mordecai'** must be distinguished from the cousin of Esther with the same name who remained in Persia when the Jews migrated back to their homeland. **'The priests'** (2:36-39) were descendants of Aaron, the first Jewish high priest and brother of Moses the law-giver

(Exod. 28; 29), whereas **'the Levites'** (2:40-42) were members of the same tribe, but not descended from the family of Aaron. Among the Levites who assisted the priests with their duties (Num. 3:5-16), were two smaller groups, **'the singers'** (2:41) and **'the gatekeepers of the temple'** (2:42). It was David who first selected some of the Levites for these special ministries (1 Chron. 25; 26). Ezra gave details about another batch of Jews, including some priests, who were unable to find their family records (2:59-63). **'The temple servants'** (2:43-54) and **'the descendants of the servants of Solomon'** (2:55-58) were comprised of non-Jews who for various reasons became part of the chosen race (e.g. war or poverty). They were considered the least important of the temple staff and undertook the menial tasks.

When we add together the numbers for the Israelite men, 24,144 (2:2-35); the priests, 4,289 (2:36-39); the Levites and the servants, 733 (2:40-58) and those who could not discover their family records, 652 (2:60), we arrive at the figure of 29,818. How does this tie in with the number given in verse 64: **'The whole company numbered 42,360'**? We must assume that the difference in the figures is because women and children are included in verse 64. A few more sums still remain. Add to the 42,360, **'7,337 menservants and maidservants'** and **'200 men and women singers'** (2:65), and the grand total works out as 49,897 people who made the journey from Babylon to Judah.

So then, what spiritual benefit may we derive from Ezra 2? It was reading the following comments of Ironside that stimulated me to take a closer look at this chapter: 'Most of the names are for us only names, but God has not forgotten one of the persons once called by these names on earth... He will reward according to the work of each... Nothing of good or ill shall be overlooked by Him who ... looks not on the outward appearance but on the heart. How little did any of these devoted Jews of Ezra's day think that God would preserve a registry of their names and families for future generations to read and thus to learn how highly He values all that is done from devotion of heart to Himself and for the glory of His name!'[1] As we go further on into the books of Ezra and Nehemiah we shall come across more of these tables of names; it will therefore be useful to keep these comments by Ironside in the back of our minds.

Ezra 2 tells us about three topics: service, holiness and giving.

Service

1. Service is varied

Service was rendered to the Lord by priests, Levites, singers, gatekeepers, temple servants and the descendants of Solomon's servants, who did the humblest service of all. Every group had its work to do in the temple and each person within the group had his allotted task to perform for the smooth running of the temple. In the temple of God's church there is a sphere of service for every Christian. Peter compares the church to a temple in which all believers are priests offering spiritual sacrifices to God (1 Peter 2:5). Paul uses a different illustration to make the same point when he compares the church to a body where every member is a limb which must function if the body is to be healthy. All the members of God's church have a gift and a ministry which they are to fulfil for the benefit of the whole body. It is in this way that the body grows and Christ the Head is glorified (1 Cor. 12).

2. Service is a privilege

It is a wonderful privilege to serve the Lord. Even the descendants of Solomon's servants, those with the lowest status of all,

were given a work to do for God in his temple. The newest
convert and the weakest Christian may labour for God in
whatever capacity the Lord may choose for him or her. Those
who feel that their toil for the Saviour is so feeble and of not
much value should realize that it is precious to him because
they are precious to him.

3. Service is for all

The temple servants and the descendants of Solomon's servants, who were not Hebrews by birth, served alongside the
Jews in the temple. God delights in the labour of all his people
regardless of their racial or social background. The priesthood
is no longer restricted to a special élite within the church, or
even to men; all believers, male and female, are priests
appointed by God. The pastor, elders and deacons have their
God-appointed rôles to fulfil, but so does every other member
of the church. The task of 'pastors and teachers' is to 'prepare
God's people for works of service, so that the body of Christ
may be built up' (Eph. 4:11-12). It is important that pastors
study diligently to preach the Bible powerfully and effec-
tively, and that elders care for the souls of saints and sinners.
Furthermore, it is vital that deacons are conscientious in their
ministry of compassion and that Sunday School teachers are
faithful in the preparation of their lessons. However, it is also
essential that the person who sweeps the place of worship does
it thoroughly as service for the Saviour. Bad sermons in the
pulpit and cobwebs in the pews are both a disgrace to the Lord!
We all have some part to play in the life of the church.
Therefore, the enquiry of the new Christian ought to be that of
Paul at his conversion: 'What shall I do, Lord?' (Acts 22:10).
The mature Christian should periodically review his or her
service and pose the question: 'Has the Lord some fresh work
for me to do?'

Holiness

We read in verses 59-63 about some Jews, among them priests, who were unsure of their family roots. This uncertainty had serious consequences for the priests, who were thus unable to establish their rights to serve in the temple. Zerubbabel, the governor, barred these men from eating the sacrificial meat until a priest could be found who knew how to discern the mind of God through the use of **'the Urim and Thummim'** (2:63).

The exact nature of 'the Urim and Thummin' is unknown, but it may have comprised two stones attached to the breastpiece of the high priest's ephod which lit up to indicate the will of God when faced with alternative courses of action (Exod. 28:15-30).[2] The implication of verse 63 is that either these stones were mislaid in the exile, or the ability to use them had been withdrawn. 'Heaven seemed to have fallen silent,' but 'The silence would soon be broken by prophecy again,'[3] when God sent Haggai and Zechariah to preach to his people (5:1).

What happened later to these priests is never stated in Scripture. Zerubbabel was acting in obedience to the commandment of Moses in the book of Numbers: 'No one except a descendant of Aaron should come to burn incense before the Lord' (Num. 16:40). 'Therefore the precautions that were now being taken were not excessive but a plain duty.'[4] The governor considered obedience to God more important than popularity with men.

The purpose of the Mosaic law was to emphasize the point that a holy God demands holiness from those who offer him worship and who profess to serve him. Just as Zerubbabel was concerned for the purity of the Jewish priesthood, so we are to be cautious about whom we allow into our pulpits and into the membership of our churches. We can only be effective in our witness to the world if we uphold the high standards which God has set for us in his Word.

Giving

The way in which the Jews gave themselves and their gifts for
the house of God is a model for us as we devote our money,
time and abilities to the Lord's work (2:68-69).

The **'drachmas of gold'** (2:69) probably refer to the
Persian daric introduced by, and named after, Darius the king.
According to the NIV footnote the drachmas weighed about
1,100 pounds or 500 kilograms, whereas the **'minas'** (2:69)
weighed about $2^4/5$ tons or 2.9 metric tons. Fifty shekels made
a mina and sixty minas made a talent.

We note three things about the giving of the new arrivals in
Jerusalem.

1. It was prompt

As soon as they arrived back in Jerusalem the Jews **'gave
freewill offerings towards the rebuilding of the house of
God'** (2:68). Time and money were earmarked for this project
even before they began to erect their own homes.

2. It was spontaneous

Their gifts were **'freewill offerings'** (2:68). They did not
require a sermon on stewardship to cajole them into parting
with their money! Our love for Christ can be measured by how
much time and money we give to him.

3. It was thoughtful

They gave **'according to their ability'** (2:69), the rich according to his riches and the poor according to his poverty. The
widow donated her two mites, which was everything that she
possessed (Mark 12:41-44). Do we plan our giving in a
systematic way related to the wages we earn?

3. It was generous

Each one contributed as much as he could. Jesus said, 'Freely you have received, freely give' (Matt. 10:8).

Will the Old Testament people of God put us to shame, who have John 3:16 in our Bibles: 'For God so loved the world that he gave his one and only Son, that whoever believes in him shall not perish but have eternal life'?

Israel's goal

The nation's quest on returning to Judah was to rebuild the temple of the Lord so that the worship of God might be restored in the land. The church is now the temple of the living God which is to be exclusively devoted to him. Our goal should be to add new stones to the temple by our godly behaviour and active evangelism. To achieve that aim we need God's might that was promised to Zerubbabel, who led the captives home: '"Not by might nor by power, but by my Spirit", says the Lord Almighty' (Zech. 4:6).

A list of names? Yes, but this is part of God's inerrant Word with a much-needed message for today concerning service, holiness and giving. A sense of excitement at a new opportunity dominates this chapter. Do we pray for new opportunities to serve the Lord?

4.
Four essential ingredients for spiritual blessing

Please read Ezra chapter 3

In an age when most people never enter the doors of a place of worship on Sundays and the majority have dismissed the church as irrelevant and outdated, it is vital for us to ask ourselves some pertinent questions. As evangelicals we claim to have the true gospel, but why are we making so little impact on the unchurched masses? What can we do to secure God's favour on our churches? Ezra 3 spells out for us the four essential ingredients for spiritual blessing. These indispensable components, which are found in every period of revival, are urgently needed today.

When the Jews returned to Jerusalem they found the temple in ruins. How did they set about restoring the worship of God and rebuilding the temple, and how can we revitalize the worship of God and build the temple of the church? We find the answers to these questions in Ezra 3. As we study this chapter, let us bear in mind that the reason for God's choice of Israel and for the existence of the church in the world is that unbelievers may have a pattern of how to worship God. The Lord's people, then and now, are God's witnesses to the unconverted (Isa. 43:10).

1. Unity

'**The people assembled as one man in Jerusalem**' (3:1). The priests, Levites and all the people met together in the capital city where the temple once stood and where their fathers formerly worshipped the Lord. They gathered with the united aim of building the temple in order to re-establish the worship of the true God.

The time and place gave them a sense of solidarity as well as reminding them of their special relationship with God. It was '**the seventh month**' (Tisri, equivalent to our September/ October in the year 537 B.C.), the month in which three of their annual religious festivals were scheduled: the Feast of Trumpets (Lev. 23:23-25), the Day of Atonement (Lev. 16) and the Feast of Tabernacles (Lev. 23:33-44). The assembly was held in Jerusalem (3:1) — the site of the holy city would bring back a flood of sacred memories to the minds of the worshippers. The timing and the location of the celebration reminded them of their identity as a distinct race separated from other nations.

Verse 9 pinpoints the unanimity of the leaders who joined together to supervise the temple-building project. Similarly, church officers ought to be a pattern of unity for the people of God.

Division hinders the growth of a church, but in our desire for concord we must not confuse biblical unity with external conformity. Inevitably there will be different gifts and ministries, in addition to variety in our social upbringing and cultural interests, plus a whole spectrum of religious experiences, all within the same local church. Therefore we should not be surprised if there is sometimes friction among church members; nevertheless it is imperative that we learn to live peaceably together so that God is glorified. We should ask ourselves, 'Does the church to which I belong practise the words of the apostle Peter: "All of you, live in harmony with

one another; be sympathetic, love as brothers, be compassionate and humble"?' (1 Peter 3:8). We ought to reflect on the
significance of the word 'brothers'. Christians who fall out
with one another are members of the same family through
God's grace. It dishonours the Lord when brothers and sisters
squabble among themselves.

2. Zeal

The Jews **'built the altar'** (3:3) before they ordered the
materials for the temple (3:7). The worship of God was a
priority placed even before the erection of a place for worship;
the preparation of our hearts is more important than the
building where we worship. The exiles did not spend time and
money on expensive homes, or take a holiday after the 900-
mile journey; neither did they wait for the temple to be
completely built before the sacrifices restarted. They determined to set their worship and their lives on a right footing
from the beginning. This is the kind of ardour that Jesus
demanded in the Sermon on the Mount: 'Seek first his kingdom and his righteousness' (Matt. 6:33). Will the fervour of
the Old Testament church put us to shame? Are we enthusiastic about the Lord's work? There are some Christians who are
slow to volunteer for work but when it comes to church
members' meetings are extremely vocal. They know exactly
how the job should be done, but they never offer to do it! Such
people are zealous with their lips but not with their hands and
feet!

The threatening situation — **'their fear of the peoples
around them'** (3:3) — did not deter the Jews from their task
of constructing the altar. The altar would in fact be a timely
reminder of the willingness of God to give them divine
assistance. The altar was the place where God had promised to
meet with his people and was the visible guarantee of his

presence: 'I will consecrate the Tent of Meeting and the altar...
Then I will dwell among the Israelites and be their God. They
will know that I am the Lord their God, who brought them out
of Egypt so that I might dwell among them. I am the Lord their
God' (Exod. 29:44-46). It often takes problems to make us
realize our need of God's help.

The zeal of the builders not only revealed itself in the way
in which they got their priorities sorted out, but also in their
giving, which was costly. In addition to their time they gave
their animals (3:5-6) and their money to the workers, plus food
to pay for the materials required (3:7). The skilled craftsmen,
the **'masons and carpenters'**, used their expertise to construct the temple (3:7) and others were willing to take on the
responsibility of supervising the project (3:8-9). The priests
and the musicians joyfully led the worship at the ceremony to
mark the laying of the foundation (3:10-11). Everyone gave
their time and their abilities, besides their possessions, to push
forward the building work, and this was done with unstinted
zest for God's glory. It is this kind of commitment which God
will bless in any local church.

As in the days of the building of Solomon's temple, the
cedar was brought in from Lebanon to the port city of Joppa,
about thirty-five miles north-west of Jerusalem (3:7; cf. 2 Chron.
2:16). **'Sidon and Tyre'** (3:7), present-day Saida and Sur
respectively, were Phoenician seaports on the coast of Lebanon. Tyre was especially well known for its astute merchants
and its slave-traders; **'Lebanon'** was famous for its forests of
myrtles, conifers and cedars; and **'Joppa'**, now known as the
port of Jaffa, was the place where Jonah boarded a ship in a
futile attempt to run away from God.

The actual work of rebuilding the temple did not begin until
**'the second month of the second year after their arrival at
the house of God in Jerusalem'** (3:8). The second month of
the Jewish sacred year was Iyar, corresponding to our April/
May. How do we explain this delay? Was their interest abating

so soon? No, God allowed his people time to adjust to their new environment. 'They needed to build houses, start farms and businesses so that they could earn a living. There is nothing unspiritual in these things themselves. It is when they take over and gain too high a priority at the exclusion of the real calling that criticism is justified.'[1] Sadly, a later generation displayed more zeal for constructing luxurious homes for themselves while God's house was in a state of disrepair (Hag. 1:2-4). Is the work of God of more concern to us than our families, home, work and leisure pursuits?

When the people were ready, **'Zerubbabel ... began the work, appointing Levites twenty years of age and older to supervise the building of the house of the Lord'** (3:8). God gave Moses instructions that Levites between the ages of twenty-five and fifty were expected to perform duties related to the meeting-place for the worship of God (Num. 8:24), but both Solomon and Zerubbabel lowered the recruitment age by five years because of the urgency of the task in hand (1 Chron. 23:24-27).

3. Obedience

The Jews built the altar (3:2), offered sacrifices (3:3-4) and celebrated the Feast of Tabernacles (3:4) in strict observance of God's own instructions given through Moses: **'Zerubbabel ... and his associates ... began to build ... in accordance with what is written in the Law of Moses the man of God'** (3:2). Nothing was permitted in the building or the ritual that was not prescribed by God's own command — a cardinal precept which every church should comply with if it is seeking the Lord's favour. It is crucial that our worship, doctrines, government, evangelism and the conduct of church members be derived from the Word of God, and not determined by our own whims and opinions. If we are to know God's blessing we must not have a low view of the Bible — that is the fast lane to apostasy. The life of the church and of every individual member is to be ruled by the inerrant Word of God. Obedience to God equals implicit obedience to his Word.

As an expression of their submission to God's Word in 'the Law of Moses the man of God' (3:2), the Jews **'sacrificed burnt offerings ... to the Lord, both the morning and evening sacrifices. Then in accordance with what is written, they celebrated the Feast of Tabernacles with the required number of burnt offerings prescribed for each day'** (3:3-4). The deliverance from seventy years of captivity in Babylon was still fresh in their minds; it was therefore appropriate that they should observe the Feast of Tabernacles, which looked back to the rescue of their forefathers from slavery in Egypt. Gratitude to God is a stimulus to obedience rendered to him. The sacrifices offered to God (3:3-6) were a confession of sin and a declaration that God alone could pardon iniquity on the basis of blood shed in the place of guilty sinners. All the Old Testament oblations pointed like signposts to Jesus Christ, the Lamb of God (John 1:29).

4. Worship

When the foundation of the temple was laid in the spring of 536 B.C. the people of God met together for worship (3:10-13). Before we go out to the world with the gospel we are to fall down in awe at the greatness of the holy God. What were the elements of the worship on that memorable occasion?

It was disciplined worship

The worship was conducted by **'the priests in their vestments'**, assisted by **'the Levites'** (3:10). The vestments worn by the Jewish priest are described in Exodus 28. God does not require those who conduct worship today to dress up in ornamental clothes; rather all believers are to 'clothe [themselves] with compassion, kindness, humility, gentleness and patience' (Col. 3:12), not just on Sunday, but on every other day of the week too. For the child of God the whole of life is 'spiritual ... worship' (Rom. 12:1).

The Jews' worship was also exuberant — **'All the people gave a great shout of praise to the Lord'** (3:11) — but orderly. Deliverance from seventy years of exile was something to get excited about!

It contained music

'The priests ... with trumpets, and the Levites ... with cymbals, took their places to praise the Lord' (3:10). The Jews' disciplined worship was certainly not dull or demure; it could hardly be so with the blast of trumpets and the crashing of cymbals! Music, like fire, is a good servant but a bad master. Music is to aid our worship but must not degenerate into entertainment.

There was singing

'With praise and thanksgiving they sang to the Lord' (3:11). The priests' song was taken from two Psalms, 118 and 136:

> **He is good;**
> **his love to Israel endures for ever.**

These same words were sung at the dedication of Solomon's temple four centuries earlier (2 Chron. 5:13; 7:3). **'They sang to the Lord'** (3:11), who alone merits our adoration. There should be nothing trivial or superficial in our worship. Our hymns ought to be worthy of the glorious God whom we adore.

However, not everyone was joyful! **'But many of the older priests and Levites and family heads, who had seen the former temple, wept aloud when they saw the foundation of this temple being laid, while many others shouted for joy. No one could distinguish the sound of the shouts of joy from the sound of weeping, because the people made so much noise. And the sound was heard far away'** (3:12-13). The older men who recalled the grandeur of Solomon's temple, destroyed about fifty years before, wept because the new temple was smaller and less magnificent. The same reaction occurred fifteen years later (Hag. 2:3). Older people may often be inclined to be too pessimistic and to live too much in the past, sometimes dampening the godly enthusiasm of the young. On the other hand, younger Christians have a tendency to be over-confident and rush ahead into a new venture without proper planning and careful thought. We need both the wisdom of age and the vigour of youth in Christian work.

To think about

1. Is there a Christian in your church with whom you have a rift?
2. Is your lack of zeal frustrating your church officers and holding back God's favour on your church?
3. How will you face your Saviour if you are refusing to obey some command of his Word?
4. Is the Saviour who poured out his blood for you more precious to you than anyone or anything else?
5. Does your worship focus attention on men or God?
6. Are you doing all you can to increase these four essential ingredients for spiritual blessing in your church?

5.
An offer refused

Please read Ezra chapter 4

'Faith which can't be tested can't be trusted.'[1] Therefore we must expect antagonism to gospel activity and to our profession of the Saviour. Whenever God initiates a spiritual work there is bound to be resistance. So it was with the people of God soon after their return from Babylon to the land of Judah. The euphoria of the foundation-stone-laying ceremony had hardly died down before their enemies launched an attack, firstly in the guise of friendship, then employing intimidation which later gave way to physical assault. It is interesting to notice that the Hebrew word translated as **'accusation'** (4:6) is related to the Greek word rendered as 'Satan' in Revelation 12:9. Satan, 'the accuser of our brothers' (Rev. 12:10), is the instigator of all human malice against Christians. However, the Lord, who is our 'shield and defender', gives us strength to resist the scheming devil and wisdom to discern his diabolical stratagems. Satan plots our downfall, but God uses the devil's cunning plans to produce in us 'a harvest of righteousness' (Heb. 12:11). Trials may become stepping-stones to bring us closer to God.

The intermingling of the Jews with the surrounding nations would soon lead to their adopting the false gods and pagan ethics of those races; therefore God allowed prolonged and bitter persecution against his own people. Trouble was a constant reminder of their weakness and of their need of the Lord's sustaining grace. The separation of God's people from the ungodly was preparing the Jewish nation for the coming of Christ. Ezra 4 traces the opening of hostilities against God's covenant people which began in the reign of King Cyrus (538-530 B.C.), continued through the reigns of Darius I (522-486 B.C.) and Xerxes (the Ahasuerus of the book of Esther, 486-465 B.C.) and on into the time of Artaxerxes (whose reign spanned the events from Ezra 7 through to the end of the book of Nehemiah, 465-424 B.C.).

It is in Ezra 4, with its reference to Persian kings, that the first Aramaic section begins, in verse 8, and runs through to Ezra 6:18. Aramaic, a language related to Hebrew but distinct from it, was used for official documents throughout the Persian empire.

The NIV heading above verse 6 reads, 'Later opposition under Xerxes and Artaxerxes,' and indicates that Ezra 4:6-23 should be in parenthesis. The clue to this fact is found in verse 12. The letter to Artaxerxes was to stop the building of **'Jerusalem ... that rebellious and wicked city'**, not to halt the building of the temple, which had been standing for half a century when Artaxerxes came to the throne. In films there is often a 'flashback' to some incident in the past, but in Ezra 4 we have a 'flash forward' to events which took place several years later. Why does Ezra include affairs in the reign of Artaxerxes in the fourth chapter of his book? 'Without that foretaste of history to reveal the full seriousness of the opposition, we should not properly appreciate the achievements recorded in the next two chapters (5 and 6), nor the dangers in the mixed marriages which Ezra would set himself to stamp out (chapters 7-10).'[2]

The offer we must refuse (4:1-3)

One day some Samaritans came to Zerubbabel and offered to
assist him in the building of the temple, but he rejected them
out of hand. We may be inclined to think that his behaviour
comes across as ungracious and abrasive, especially as the
offer may have been sincerely meant and would certainly have
eased the workload of the Jews. The description of these
Samaritans in verse 1, as **'enemies of Judah'**, explains
Zerubbabel's reaction and alerts us to a concealed danger in
what appears as a harmless proposal. The devil's temptations,
like the offer of the Samaritans, sometimes lurk behind the
warmth of apparent friendship.

These Samaritans were descendants of the conquered races
that the Assyrians had transported to Israel in 721 B.C. (2 Kings
17:24-28). They intermarried with the few Israelites left in the
land after the exile and thus formed a hybrid race. Their religion was a hotchpotch of idol-worship and Jehovah-worship
(2 Kings 17:24-41). We read in 2 Kings 17:33 that 'They
worshipped the Lord, but they also served their own gods in
accordance with the customs of the nations from which they
had been brought.' These intruders did not really know the
Lord at all and would have led the Jews back into idolatry. The
veneration of idols was one of the sins which resulted in the
seventy years of exile. It was therefore imperative for
Zerubbabel on behalf of the people of God to refuse the
volunteer labour of the Samaritans. The Judean governor cites
the authority of the Persian king and the greater authority of
God as he turns down the Samaritans' proposal: **'You have no
part with us in building a temple to our God. We alone will
build it for the Lord, the God of Israel, as King Cyrus, the
king of Persia, commanded us'** (4:3).

There is an offer that we too must refuse: it is the suggestion
that we compromise with unbelievers. 'I'll give you ease and

pleasure if you are not so strict and rigorous in your religion,' the devil whispers in our ears. He will frequently use the voices of those we love in our families who are not Christians. It is becoming increasingly difficult for the Christian in the secularized and materialistic world of today because he is under constant pressure to tone down his convictions so that he can get along more easily with non-Christian relatives and colleagues. The New Testament warning against the danger of compromise is clearly stated by the apostle Paul in 2 Corinthians 6:14: 'Do not be yoked together with unbelievers.' The Christian is not to be discourteous, or detached from unbelievers; rather he is to befriend them to gain an opening to present the gospel, but he ought never to keep their friendship by compromising his convictions. The words of Paul forbid unethical business deals and emotional entanglements with unbelievers. Believers are not to date and marry non-Christians because this is a sure way of getting drawn away from the Saviour.

As evangelicals we are to stand outside the ecumenical movement. The relevance of Ezra 4 to the ecumenical scene is clear from the fact that the Samaritans, whose offer Zerubbabel rejected, were religious and more than willing to worship the Jewish God alongside their own gods. They, like the ecumenists, were amicable until crossed! Ezra 4 teaches us that Christians are distinct from non-Christians. Nothing must be allowed to blur that distinction.

Another important application from this chapter is that only Christians are qualified to serve the Lord. The Samaritans' proposition was repudiated because they did not really belong to the Lord. If a church permits into its membership unconverted people it will not be long before their unspiritual thinking contaminates the whole church. They could rise to positions of leadership and promote worldly activities and unbiblical teaching. Zerubbabel detected the insincerity of the Samaritans; in the same manner pastors and elders need discernment to perceive hypocrisy and error. They are to display courage as they apply firm, caring discipline when deception and heresy are discovered.

The trouble we cannot avoid (4:4-23)

When churches and Christians maintain these two principles, that Christians are distinct from non-Christians and that Christians only are qualified to serve the Lord, then unbelievers will marshal their forces against them. The Samaritans changed their tune once their offer was spurned; then they became the bitter enemies of God's people. These Samaritans found willing allies in **'the peoples around'** — the non-Jewish inhabitants, not only of Samaria, but also of Judah, Idumea and the surrounding districts — as they sought to **'discourage the people of Judah and make them afraid to go on building'** (4:4). The word 'discourage' in the Hebrew contains the meaning of 'to weaken the hands'.

1. This attack on the Jews was menacing (4:5)

They intimidated the temple-builders and employed professional help, **'counsellors'**, to discredit their victims before the authorities. A similar tactic was later used in an attempt to frighten Nehemiah so that he would desert his work and thus be branded as a coward by God's people (Neh. 6:10-13). Nehemiah was not scared off by this threatening behaviour. In situations such as these we may rest on the promise of God's presence. 'God has said, "Never will I leave you; never will I forsake you". So we may say with confidence, "The Lord is my helper; I will not be afraid. What can man do to me?"' (Heb. 13:5-6).

2. The attack was persistent (4:5-7)

Sadly, the temple-builders were not as thick-skinned and as resolute as Nehemiah, who built the city walls in a mere fifty-two days, much to the consternation of his opponents (Neh. 6:15-16). The temple-building work which began with enthusiasm in 536 B.C., in the reign of Cyrus, came to an abrupt stop a few months afterwards. The project was eventually completed twenty-two years later in the reign of Darius. The persecution of the Jews which began in the days of Cyrus dragged on for over eighty years into the reigns of Darius, Xerxes and Artaxerxes. Relentless conflict and intense temptation are like water that wears away the stone. Our tender-hearted God has promised his people that 'Your strength will equal your days... The eternal God is your refuge, and underneath are the everlasting arms' (Deut. 33:25,27).

3. The attack was powerful (4:7-10)

The highest officials joined forces to exterminate God's work. An impressive list of names was cited in Rehum's letter to Artaxerxes to impress the monarch. As we have already noted, the passage from 4:8 - 6:18 is the first of the two Aramaic sections found in the book of Ezra. **'Ashurbanipal'** (4:10) was Osnappar, the Assyrian sovereign who ruled from 669-626 B.C., and the **'Trans-Euphrates'** (4:10) was the region west of the Euphrates which included Syria and Palestine. All the united powers of men and devils cannot destroy the church which Christ built on himself (Matt. 16:18).

4. The attack was cunning (4:12-16)

A three-pronged appeal was made to Artaxerxes: Rehum, as the spokesperson of the other officials, claimed that, if the

Jews were not prevented from building the city of Jerusalem,
the king would suffer financially (4:13) and his honour would
be damaged (4:14) through the loss of some of his kingdom
(4:15-16). This was an absurd exaggeration because not since
the days of Solomon had Israel controlled land all the way to
the Euphrates river, which flows through Iraq (1 Kings 4:21).
Years later Jesus gave to his disciples a warning about the
deviousness of the wicked: 'I am sending you out like sheep
among wolves. Therefore be as shrewd as snakes and as
innocent as doves' (Matt. 10:16).

5. The attack was zealous and brutal (4:23)

The words, **'They went immediately to the Jews in Jerusalem,'** show their wicked zeal and the fact that they **'compelled
them by force to stop'** unmasks their brutality as they made
the building of the city come to a standstill. The letter of King
Artaxerxes gave Rehum and his associates the trump card, and
they knew it! (4:17-22).

    Christians can brace themselves for hostility by reminding
themselves of their *present power* and *future glory,* of which
we read in the New Testament: 'Be strong in the Lord and in
his mighty power' (Eph. 6:10); and 'I consider that our present
sufferings are not worth comparing with the glory that will be
revealed in us' (Rom. 8:18).

The example we should not follow (4:24)

Verse 24 follows chronologically after verse 5. We are now
back in the days of Zerubbabel and the reign of Cyrus. It is a
sad fact that the intimidation of the Samaritans persuaded the
people of God to abandon their building project for sixteen
years until 520 B.C. Though this is an understandable response to incessant harassment it is certainly not an example

to copy. Coleman Luck makes a perceptive assessment of the Jews' predicament at that time: 'While not minimizing the peril of their situation, it is evident from Haggai's prophecy that their own enthusiasm for the work had also waned. There is no evidence that they carried the matter any further, either by prayer to God or by petition to the king. We are forced to conclude that they capitulated too easily. All too often believers in our own day do the same, giving up with hardly a struggle when opposition arises against the Lord's work.'[3] Those who are on the brink of resigning from some Christian ministry through discouragement should remind themselves that it is too soon to quit! Whatever stress and strain Christians are under, they should not give Satan the victory by relinquishing their post of duty.

6.
Coping with discouragement

Please read Ezra chapter 5

As we turn from Ezra 4 into chapter 5 we move on fourteen years from the reign of Cyrus to that of Darius I. Cyrus was killed during a battle in 530 B.C. and was succeeded by his son Cambyses, who put his brother Smerdis to death and conquered Egypt in 527 or 525 B.C. There is some uncertainty surrounding the death of Cambyses: some historians suggest that he committed suicide and others that he died as the result of an accident. Darius came to the throne in 522 and reigned until 486 B.C. He was a Persian by birth and brought up in Zoroastrianism, which is based on the concept of an ongoing struggle between good and evil. Darius established this religion as the state religion of Persia.

The mood of God's people at this time was one of abject depression. The people were so downhearted that they abandoned their attempt to renovate the temple. They never wanted to see another brick or trowel (4:24). The two prophets, Haggai and Zechariah, had their work cut out as they tried to cure the cancer of discouragement which was raging among the Jews. Most Christians feel dejected at some time or the other in the Lord's work. There are Sunday evenings when the pastor vows never to preach another sermon and when Sunday School teachers are ready to quit their class. Deacons grow weary of their duties in the midst of their busy lives. The footsore door-to-door visitor wonders if all his efforts are really worthwhile after a street-full of people politely refuse to engage in spiritual conversation. Ezra 5 can teach us how to cope with discouragement.

The preaching of Haggai and Zechariah (5:1-2)

God did not forsake his people in their dejection or leave them to wallow in their self-pity. Instead he sent two prophets to spur them on to action: **'Haggai ... and Zechariah ... prophesied to the Jews in Judah... Then Zerubbabel ... and Jeshua ... set to work.'** The effective remedy to discouragement was the bold proclamation of the Word of God. These men were the first prophets sent by God to Israel since Daniel, who had prophesied sixteen years before in the third year of Cyrus (Dan. 10:1).

Zechariah is introduced as **'a descendant of Iddo'** (5:1). The prophet himself opens his own book by informing us that he was the 'son of Berekiah, the son of Iddo' (Zech. 1:1), so Iddo was his grandfather.

Haggai began his ministry two months before Zechariah (compare Hag. 1:1 with Zech. 1:1). Haggai preached four sermons within the space of three months in 520 B.C. and then disappeared from public view. His short ministry was certainly a productive one!

Ironside helpfully draws a picture of the biblical prophet: 'The true prophet is the one whose words come from heaven to men on earth, searching the heart, reaching the conscience and exposing the evil that may have come in.'[1] Though preaching (which requires study) is different from prophecy (a direct message from God), Ironside's words are a good 'job description' of the preacher's task in these days.

Both Haggai and Zechariah preached with *the authority of God* — they **'prophesied to the Jews ... in the name of the God of Israel'** — and in *the power of God* — **'the God of**

Israel, who was over them' (5:1). Nevertheless their styles of
preaching were distinctly different. Haggai rebuked and reproved in clear, plain language and did not mince his words,
whereas Zechariah, who encouraged the people, was in the
words of Kidner 'enigmatic and visionary'.[2] The church always needs preachers with fearless courage who can inspire
believers with far-reaching vision and exuberant vitality for
the cause of God. In the life of a church there will often be a
variety of spiritual leaders with a diversity of gifts which ought
to be put to use for the benefit of all the members. All forms
of ministry — one pastor or many elders, an approach like that
of Haggai or a style like that of Zechariah — will be unfruitful
without the favour of God.

It was God alone who made the joint service of Haggai and
Zechariah successful among the Hebrews. It was no easy task
to get the people of God working again, especially in the light
of Haggai's own evaluation of the situation that many of them
had been caught in the snare of worldliness. Worldliness may
be defined as 'that state in which our thinking is governed by
the mind and outlook of the world'. In the Bible the word
'world' is frequently used to mean 'the world of unbelievers'.
Haggai tells us in the first chapter of his prophecy that the Jews
were building themselves luxurious houses and neglecting the
house of God. Their time and energy spent on themselves and
their occupations had produced so little because of inflation:
'You have planted much, but have harvested little. You eat,
but never have enough. You drink, but never have your fill.
You put on clothes, but are not warm. You earn wages, only
to put them in a purse with holes in it' (Hag. 1:6). The Jews,
God's own people, were governed by 'the mind and outlook
of the world', but God was frustrating their craving for
possessions and a life of ease.

What a contrast to the euphoria displayed some sixteen
years before when they first returned to Israel! How the years

had taken their toll! Discouragement bred idleness, which in turn gave birth to worldliness. Is the same true of ourselves? We ought periodically to ask ourselves questions such as, 'Do I have the same fervour for the Lord's work that I had when first converted, or has the rot of disillusionment and worldliness eaten its way into my soul?' In days gone by the Bible was avidly read and prayer a delight. Once the prayer meeting was never missed and preaching was food to our souls, but now worldliness has drained away spiritual vitality. Worldliness is a constant temptation to Christians living in a materialistic age.

Do you remember from your childhood the stories of Sinbad the sailor? In one of those stories Sinbad was sailing in the Indian Ocean when a magnetic rock rose from the surface of the placid waters. Sinbad's vessel was sucked irresistibly towards it. One by one the bolts were drawn out of the ship's side and the whole structure of bulwarks, masts and spars tumbled into ruin on the sea. So the sailors woke to find themselves drowning in the ocean. Worldliness has an enchanting attraction; bolt after bolt of good resolutions, clamp after clamp of obedience to God are gradually pulled away from the Christian; the result is backsliding. Spiritual leaders, like Haggai and Zechariah, are to warn of the subtle dangers of worldliness, which is fatal to God's people.

The outcome of the preaching of Haggai and Zechariah was that the Jews restarted the temple-building, encouraged and assisted by the two prophets: **'Zerubbabel ... and Jeshua ... set to work to rebuild... And the prophets of God were with them, helping them'** (5:2). The prophets who had faithfully administered the painful medicine of reproof to the discouraged Jews now worked alongside them in the building project. In the same way church officers are to teach their fellow church members how to serve the Lord by their own example (1 Peter 5:2-3).

We read that Zerubbabel and Jeshua, mentioned in 4:3, were still taking the lead in the renovation programme: 'Zerubbabel ... and Jeshua ... set to work to rebuild' (5:2). In the view of Haggai, Zerubbabel was the most prominent person in Judah at that time (Hag. 1:1,12,14; 2:2,4,21,23). The term used by Haggai ('governor', Hag. 1:2,14; 2:2,21) makes it clear that Zerubbabel was an official appointed by the Persians with responsibility for Judah.

The enquiry of Tattenai (5:3-5)

Once the temple-building was under way again two Persian officials, **'Tattenai, governor of Trans-Euphrates, and Shethar-Bozenai'** and a formidable group of associates appeared in Jerusalem to conduct an investigation (5:3). Secular history records that a man named Ushtani was the governor or satrap of Trans-Euphrates (the region west of the river Euphrates), at this time, so presumably Tattenai was a high official responsible to the satrap. Nevertheless he came into Jerusalem with the full backing of the Persian regime behind him. The question he put to the Jews was: **'Who authorized you to rebuild this temple and restore this structure?'** (5:3).

Why was a Persian so interested in the building of a Jewish temple? What was all the fuss about? Perhaps the Samaritans, still disgruntled because they were not allowed to assist in the building programme (4:1-5), were angry that the diligent Jews were 'making rapid progress' (5:8) in erecting the temple. Did they suggest that the 'large stones' were actually being used to build a fortress?

Another reason for this enquiry was the political situation within the empire, which had been seething with revolt throughout the two years of Darius' reign. Was this local burst of activity a further revolt in the making, a sinister plot under the guise of building a place of worship?

There is some variation in the translation of verse 4. In the NIV it reads as a request from the governor: **'What are the names of the men constructing this building?'** The New King James Version states the answer of the Jews: **'We told them the names of the men who were constructing this building,'** which implies that the question given in the NIV had been asked (cf. 5:9-10). If the NIV translation is correct then it indicates that Tattenai wanted the names of the 'ring-leaders' so that he could arrest them if this was the command of Darius.

It is instructive to consider the courteous reply of the Jews to the question of Tattenai. The governor held his office by the decree of God and was therefore given respect. It is a disgrace to Christ and the church when a Christian is rude and rebellious towards those in authority (see Rom. 13:1-2; Col. 4:5-6; 1 Peter 2:13-14).

Tattenai did not order the Jews to stop building, but only to explain their authority for the work; therefore they carried on with the project. Now they had set in motion the temple-building they were not going to be intimidated into halting once more. God himself was observing their activity to defend them: **'But the eye of their God was watching over the elders of the Jews, and they were not stopped until a report could go to Darius and his written reply be received'** (5:5). Ultimately they were answerable to God, not to Tattenai the governor, or to Darius the king. God's love for his people made even the most timid person brave. Verse 5 is a wonderful antidote to discouragement — the Lord is always watching over those who serve him faithfully! (cf. Zech. 3:9; 4:10 which also refer to the eye of God). The reference to 'the eye of God' may be 'a play on words because the Persian civil inspectors were known at that time as "the king's eye".'[3]

The letter to Darius (5:6-17)

In his letter to the Persian king Tattenai reported how he came
to Judea, and found the temple being built with large stones
and timber. He called the building under construction **'the
temple of the great God'** (5:8); though he believed in many
deities he at least recognized that Jehovah was very important.
Tattenai quotes the Jews' own description of themselves as
'the servants of the God of heaven and earth' who were
reconstructing the temple that **'a great king of Israel'** (Solomon) **'built many years ago'** (5:11).

If they were 'servants of the God of heaven and earth', why
had he allowed the temple to be destroyed and his subjects
taken captive to Babylon in the first place? The Jews had
supplied the governor with the answer to that question: **'Our
fathers angered the God of heaven'** (5:12). 'The exiles are
not blaming their forefathers in order to exonerate *themselves.*
Rather the tone of their words shows that they have taken to
heart the rebuke of Haggai and include themselves in the
punishment. The recognition of guilt is the first step in their
rediscovery of their identity as the people of God.'[4]

The Jews argued that Cyrus had decreed that they should
refurbish the temple and that he had handed back the holy
vessels taken by Nebuchadnezzar (5:13-16). Tattenai requested
King Darius to search the official records to ascertain whether
the report of the decree was correct or not, and then to send him
instructions relating to the Jews (5:17). It is interesting to
observe that the tenor of Tattenai's letter to Darius was
subdued compared with that of Rehum to Artaxerxes (4:9-16).

To pray about

Several items for prayer emerge from Ezra 5:

1. Pray that pastors/elders may know how to encourage and when to reprove.

2. Pray that God's people may be alert to the subtle attractions of worldliness.

3. Pray for winsomeness when unbelievers oppose those who work for the Lord.

4. Pray for grace to continue in the Lord's work despite all discouragements.

7.
The temple completed

Please read Ezra chapter 6

How difficult it is to await the arrival of an important letter —
for example, examination results, or the offer of a new job! Our
patience wears thin. The Jews must have felt some apprehen-
sion about the reply Tattenai would receive to the letter he
despatched to the powerful Persian king Darius. Would Darius
bother to search the old dusty records and back up the claim of
the Jews that Cyrus had commanded them to build their temple
in Jerusalem? Some of the Jews may have been dreading the
answer from Darius. Perhaps they feared that the king would
compel them to stop building. Derek Kidner sees in the
favourable response of the Persian king 'a striking instance of
the truth'[1] expressed in the hymn by William Cowper:

Ye fearful saints, fresh courage take,
The clouds ye so much dread
Are big with mercy, and shall break
In blessing on your head.[2]

Are we afraid of something that might happen in the future?
It may be an operation, redundancy, unemployment, family
problems — the list is as vast as our imaginations! God may
surprise us and turn the terrifying prospect into a blessing in
disguise. Whatever happens, whether the future is better or

worse than we imagined, it will be planned by our wise and loving heavenly Father. The God who cared for his anxious people awaiting the reply of King Darius watches over us and plans the path ahead.

The letter from Darius (6:1-12)

When King Darius eventually received the letter from Tattenai he considered the contents serious enough to order a search of the archives for the decree of Cyrus cited by the Jews. The vastness of the Persian empire caused some delay in locating the relevant document relating to the construction of the Jerusalem temple. The thoroughness of the search was evidence that Darius wanted to deal fairly with the Jews. After a fruitless search in the record house at Babylon, the elusive decree was discovered at the king's summer palace at Ecbatana, the ancient capital of Media, modern Hamadan on the road from Baghdad to Teheran in northern Iran. Ecbatana, 6,000 feet above sea level, was a cold place in winter but delightful during the rest of the year and was therefore regarded as an ideal summer home by several of the Persian kings.

The decree confirmed that Cyrus had commanded the Jews to rebuild the temple at Jerusalem and stated that the enterprise was to be financed from the king's own funds (6:4). The dimensions of the temple were to be **'ninety feet high and ninety feet wide** [27 metres high and wide] **with three courses of large stones'** (6:3-4). When we compare Ezra 6 with 1 Kings 6:2-6 we realize that the proposed size of the temple was double the height and three times the width of Solomon's temple. Cyrus' plans to excel Solomon's temple did not come to fruition and this may explain the disappointment of some of the older Jews who wept that the new temple was not as impressive as Solomon's structure (cf. 3:12; Hag.

2:3). The smaller construction may have been because the funds promised by Cyrus never materialized. The 'large stones' could now be laid with the full authority of no less a person than the exalted King of Persia! (5:8; 6:4). Darius also ordered that **'the gold and silver articles'** stolen by King Nebuchadnezzar should **'be returned to their places in the temple in Jerusalem'** (6:5).

It is evident from inscriptions on building work undertaken by Darius that he had a high regard for his predecessor Cyrus. Hence he upheld the decree of Cyrus issued eighteen years prior to its rediscovery in the archives. Darius added to it a proclamation of his own in which he reaffirmed Zerubbabel's position as **'the governor of the Jews'** (6:7) and gave Tattenai four directives (6:6-12).

1. Promote the work (6:6-7)

God used a pagan king to protect his people. Though the Bible teaches that the state and the church are to remain separate entities (Matt. 22:21), God may sometimes grant his church favour with earthly monarchs and human authorities to further his own sovereign purposes. Remember that the preservation of the Jewish race was an essential link in the chain which led to the birth in Bethlehem of the Lord Jesus Christ to a young Jewish couple, Mary and Joseph. Our salvation hinged on the safety of God's people in the days of King Darius! Furthermore, the historical events of Ezra chapter 6 are evidence that Romans 8:28 is true: 'We know that in all things God works for the good of those who love him, who have been called according to his purposes.'

2. Provide money and animals for the Jews (6:8-10)

The expenses were covered from taxes normally sent to Darius (6:4). 'In this way the people themselves had no additional taxes to pay — the king would simply get less.'³ The king's reply now put the temple-builders in a far stronger position than before.

3. Pray for the king (6:10)

Darius requests that Tattenai ask the Jews to pray for the well-being of himself and his sons. He 'was keen to be mentioned in despatches to God'.⁴ It was the policy of Darius to support the local gods throughout his kingdom to keep the majority of his citizens on his side. The support of Darius for the Jews' venture was also an act of political expediency. His defeat of the Egyptians was recent history; therefore it was necessary to have loyal subjects so close to Egypt, a difficult country to control.

Christians are commanded by God, through the apostle Paul, that 'prayers ... be made for everyone — for kings and all those in authority, that we may live peaceful and quiet lives in all godliness and holiness' (1 Tim. 2:1-2). The request for 'peaceful and quiet lives' is not a selfish desire, but rather a petition that circumstances may be advantageous for the spread of the gospel.

4. Punish those who violate the royal decree (6:11-12)

Anyone who tampered with the erection of the temple was to be impaled on a timber from his own house so that the offender was made a public spectacle to deter other potential vandals. Darius called on God to destroy any person, either ruler or private individual, who prevented the temple from being built. This edict of the king, which reflects the characteristic cruelty of Persian justice, was no idle threat. Darius had impaled 3,000 Babylonians to crush a rebellion.⁵

McConville elucidates the king's appeal to God in verse 12: **'May God, who has caused his Name to dwell there,**

overthrow any king or people who lifts a hand to change this decree or to destroy this temple in Jerusalem.' He comments: 'He takes pains to "co-opt" the God of Israel, little thinking that the dwelling of God's Name at Jerusalem was of a significance which would outlast him, or that the Name would one day in Jerusalem, by an act of self-sacrifice which Darius could not have understood, initiate an Empire which would know no end.'[6]

The temple completed (6:13-22)

The temple was completed at long last in 515 B.C., **'on the third day of the month Adar, in the sixth year of the reign of King Darius'** (6:15). Adar corresponds to our March. It was the sixth month of the Jewish civil year and the final month of their religious calendar. The 'sixth year of the reign of King Darius', according to Jewish reckoning, would have extended from Nisan (April) 516 to Adar 515 B.C. The temple was completed about seventy years after the destruction of Solomon's temple, twenty-one years after the laying of the foundation-stone and about four and half years after Haggai and Zechariah's preaching to the discouraged builders (Ezra 5). Solomon's temple stood for four hundred years; the rebuilt temple was replaced by Herod's temple, begun in 19 B.C. and destroyed by the Roman emperor Titus in A.D. 70. The completion of the temple gave back to the Jews a focal point, a visible symbol of their identity as the chosen people of God. The cornerstone of the church, God's temple, is Christ, who unites the 'living stones' and gives them identity as his people (1 Peter 2:4-10; Eph. 2:19-22).

This section of Ezra chapter 6 divides into three segments.

1. Completion (6:13-15)

The temple was finished through the encouragement of the Persian kings and officials, the elders of Israel and the preaching of the two prophets, Haggai and Zechariah. King Artaxerxes is mentioned in verse 14 though he reigned from 465 to 424 B.C., fifty years after the temple was erected. He later contributed money to 'honour the house of the Lord' (7:20,27). The New King James Version translates the word 'honour' (7:27) as 'beautify'; the Persian king desired that the Jews' temple should be attractive and pleasing to the eyes of all who worshipped within its walls. Artaxerxes' gifts for the temple were carried to Jerusalem by Ezra.

In spite of the gloomy catalogue of opposition in Ezra 4 the plan of God had been fulfilled and the power of God had defeated all foes. Everything was done **'according to the command of ... God'**, but nothing was done apart from human effort (6:14). God works in history but he uses human instruments (even unconverted men such as Darius) and human events (even bringing good out of evil) to accomplish his decrees.

2. Dedication (6:16-18)

This dedication is reminiscent of that of Solomon's temple (2 Chron. 7). The people of God **'celebrated the dedication of the house of God with joy'** (6:16). This reference to joy is all the more notable when compared with the despondency of the previous years. The word 'joy' has not occurred since chapter 3:13, some fourteen years earlier! We can be so preoccupied with our problems that we forget to thank God for his gifts to us. The source of all true and lasting joy is the Lord:

'The Lord had filled them with joy' (6:22). In verse 22 the word for joy has the meaning of 'enjoying yourself' — that is not the usual idea which people have of Christians and the worship of God, is it?

When we compare the sacrifices offered at the dedication of Solomon's temple (1 Kings 8:63) with the offerings presented to God at the dedication of Zerubbabel's temple, those of the returned exiles seem few indeed (6:17-18). Solomon offered 22,000 cattle, compared with the 100 bullocks of the resettled Jews. Solomon slew a mixture of 120,000 sheep and goats, whereas the exiles offered **'two hundred rams, four hundred male lambs and, as a sin offering for all Israel, twelve male goats, one for each of the tribes of Israel'**. We ought, however, to remember that Solomon was an exceedingly wealthy monarch who gave out of his abundance. Though the Jews were not poor (1:5-8, 2:66-67), their giving could in no way match that of Solomon; nevertheless each person gave according to his ability.

This is exactly how God requires us all to give to his work: 'On the first day of every week, each one of you should set aside a sum of money in keeping with his income' (1 Cor. 16:2). Our 'sin offering' is not a dead animal but the living Saviour who willingly gave himself as an atonement for sin at Calvary. We ought therefore to give more to the Lord's work and praise God more than these Old Testament saints did!

The 'twelve male goats' (6:17) 'make it plain that representatives of all these tribes were present and that the full nation was still viewed as consisting not of one or two but of twelve tribes'.[7] The same point is made in verse 16 where the nation is described as **'the people of Israel'**. The priests and the Levites were fully established in their official duties, **'according to what is written in the Book of Moses'** (6:18; cf. Exod. 28; 29).

3. Celebration (6:19-22)

At verse 19 the text reverts from Aramaic to Hebrew. Shortly
after the dedication ceremony there was a memorable celebration of the Passover (6:19-21; cf. Exod. 12) and the Feast
of Unleavened Bread (6:22; cf. Lev. 23:4-8) in the new temple,
beginning on the first day of the sacred year and the seventh
month of the civil year Abib, equal to our April. It was
appropriate that **'the Israelites who had returned from the
exile'** (6:21) should eat the Passover which looked back to
their deliverance from captivity in Egypt. The priests and the
Levites who conducted the celebrations had to be **'ceremoni-
ally clean'** (6:20). The holy God can only be worshipped by
those who have 'clean hands and a pure heart' (Ps. 24:4). We
must repent of sin and reform our conduct, otherwise God will
not receive our adoration.

The Jews and the Gentile proselytes to Judaism worshipped
together and ate the Passover as one nation; unitedly they
worshipped **'the Lord, the God of Israel'** (6:21). They
separated from those who were insincere, such as the Samaritans (Ezra 4), and refused to participate in the impurity of the
Gentiles in order to enjoy fellowship with the bona fide
children of God. We must reject the spurious unity of
ecumenism; nevertheless we ought to foster zealously close
fellowship with all genuine Christians. Just as the basis of
fellowship was the shed blood of the Passover lamb, so our
fellowship is based on the blood of Christ, our Paschal Lamb
(John 1:29; 1 Cor. 5:7).

The intention of fellowship is **'to seek the Lord'** (6:21).
When we meet with fellow believers in public worship there
ought to be an earnest seeking of the Lord which will be
expressed as we sing our hymns with enthusiasm and listen
attentively to the reading and preaching of God's Word. It is

all too easy to settle into the routine of worship and to chat after worship about anything but spiritual topics.

Verse 22, with its emphasis on the sovereign might of God, forms a fitting conclusion to the chapter: **'The Lord had filled them with joy by changing the attitude of the king of Assyria, so that he assisted them in the work on the house of God, the God of Israel.'** Darius, King of Persia, is titled 'the King of Assyria', because Assyria, the former enemy of Israel, had been conquered by the Persians whose king was a friend of Israel. What had brought about this remarkable change? The Lord who directs the hearts of all men had changed the attitude of Darius so that he encouraged them in the temple-building enterprise. Evil and good men serve the eternal purposes of God. Bad times and good times are all part of his predestined plans. To use the words of the wise preacher:

> When times are good, be happy;
>   but when times are bad, consider:
> God has made the one
>   as well as the other
>
> (Eccl. 7:14).

We are to trust and obey God whether the days are good or bad.

8.
Ezra's self-portrait

Please read Ezra chapter 7

We are already six chapters into the book of Ezra and the man who did so much to shape the life of the Jewish nation has not yet appeared in the book that bears his name. At last, in chapter 7, Ezra walks on to the stage as he enters the city of Jerusalem with a fresh batch of emigrant Jews from Babylon. Meanwhile Judah has been repossessed and the temple refurbished by the exiles who returned eighty years ago in the days of Zerubbabel the governor and Cyrus the Persian king. The scene is set for Ezra 'to begin to rebuild the people of God into a nation of spiritual power and purity for the sake of the glory of God.'[1]

Fifty-seven years have elapsed between the events of chapter 6 and those of chapter 7. The year is now 458 B.C., the seventh year of the reign of Artaxerxes, son of Xerxes I, who divorced Queen Vashti and later married Esther the Jewess. Artaxerxes' friendliness to the Jews may have been the result of the influence of Esther and her cousin Mordecai, and also because of his respect for Ezra. We find evidence of the king's esteem for Ezra in the statement of verse 6: **'The king had granted him everything he asked.'**

The suppression of a revolt in Egypt was still fresh in King Artaxerxes' memory, so it was in his interests to ensure that the political situation in Judah was stable and its population loyal. To further this end he granted Ezra permission to lead another

group of Jews back to Jerusalem. The outcome of this permission was that **'Ezra arrived in Jerusalem in the fifth
month of the seventh year of the king. He had begun his
journey from Babylon on the first day of the first month,
and he arrived in Jerusalem on the first day of the fifth
month, for the gracious hand of his God was on him'** (7:8-
9). The first month was Nisan (March/April) and the fifth
month was Ab (July/August); therefore Ezra's journey began
in the spring and was completed in midsummer, fourteen
weeks later.

Ezra ascribes the king's favour and his safe arrival in
Jerusalem to the **'hand of the Lord his God ... on him'**
(7:6,9). The motif, 'the hand of the Lord', is heard several
times in chapters 7 and 8 and again in the book of Nehemiah
(Ezra 7:6,9,28; 8:18; Neh. 2:8,18). It was God who planned the
political events in Persia so that King Artaxerxes granted Ezra
his request to travel to Judah. It was the special favour of God
which kept Ezra and his travelling companions safe on the
long, dangerous journey to Jerusalem. Ezra was the man whom
God had chosen to care for his own people and to restore them
to fellowship with himself, and to forward his long-term plan
to bring salvation to sinners through the death of his Son. In a
similar way, the life of each Christian and the witness of every
local church slots into God's eternal timetable.

Ezra was **'a teacher'** (7:6), translated as 'scribe' in the
Authorized Version, and a **'priest'** (7:12). A teacher/scribe
was often employed to write letters and draw up legal documents. Examples of this are found in Jeremiah 32:11-12;
36:26. It is clear from chapter 7 that Ezra was a gifted and
effective teacher of God's law. Do we want God to use us for
the benefit of his people and the glory of his name? Then we
need to study the life of Ezra. It is men and women with the
qualities of Ezra that God will use. Sometimes when a person
fills in an application form for a job he is asked to provide a

curriculum vitae (c.v.) in which he gives details of his edu-
cational attainments, previous employment and relevant work
experience. Ezra 7 is the scribe's spiritual 'c.v', in which he
shares with us, without any pride, the qualifications with
which God equipped him for leadership among the Jews. A
prayerful study of Ezra's self-portrait could have far-reaching
consequences in our lives and for the churches of which we are
members.

Ezra's ancestry (7:1-5)

Ezra traces his family tree back to Aaron, the high priest and
brother of Moses, to prove that he was a true priest and had the
right to introduce necessary reforms. It was Moses who
originally led God's people to Israel, the land to which the
Jews were now returning with Ezra as their guide. He acted as
a second Moses in the nation. Just as God gave his law through
Moses, so Ezra 'stamped Israel with its lasting character as the
people of a book'.[2] It was God's Word which he expounded to
the people and to which he constantly demanded obedience
(7:6,10; cf. Neh. 8). It is a great privilege to have a godly
upbringing, like Ezra; however, it would be tragic if we
disgraced our ancestry by turning away from the God of our
family. We would be wise to make Ezra our model, who
'devoted himself to the study and observance of the Law of the
Lord', and to following his example to teach 'its decrees and
laws' to those who are not so favoured as ourselves (7:10).

Ezra's attainments (7:6-10)

Ezra **'came up from Babylon'** (7:6), a dangerous and gruel-
ling journey of over 900 miles, the trailblazer of several

thousand people. He knew even before the trek to Judah got under way that the task to which God had commissioned him was an onerous one. Chapters 9 and 10 give us an insight into the enormous problems he faced because the Jews in Judah had become backslidden and despondent. Ezra was not looking for the easy option; the tougher the job the better for this valiant man. Presumably Zerubbabel, the Judean governor, and Jeshua, the Jewish high priest, were now dead as they are not mentioned in the remaining chapters of Ezra; so he could not depend on their support. It is Christians of the calibre of Ezra who will see fruit from their efforts for the Lord.

Ezra accomplished so much for the Lord because of his *confidence in God's Word.* We read that **'He was a teacher well versed in the Law of Moses, which the Lord, the God of Israel, had given'** (7:6), and that **'Ezra had devoted himself to the study and observance of the Law of the Lord'** (7:10). He knew the Scriptures, obeyed them and taught them. The words 'well versed' (7:6) mean that he was quick to grasp God's message and perceive its application for his own life and for the people of God — an essential attribute for those who teach God's Word. Ezra 'devoted himself' to the study of the Law because he was convinced that it was 'the Law of Moses, which the Lord ... had given' (7:6). God had spoken and therefore Ezra must listen and obey. But God's words were written down by the pen of Moses. This doctrine of the dual human and divine authorship of the Bible is explained by Paul in 2 Timothy 3:16-17 and by Peter in 2 Peter 1:19-21. If this is how Ezra esteemed the small portion of the Bible that he possessed, how much more should we love the completed canon of God's Word?

Ezra's confidence in the Word of God makes him a pattern for us. 'He is a model reformer in that what he taught he had first lived, and what he had lived he had first made sure of in the Scriptures. With study, conduct and teaching put deliberately in this right order, each of these was able to function properly at its best: study was saved from unreality, conduct from uncertainty, and teaching from insincerity and shallowness.'[3] Ezra is a superb example of what the apostle Paul had in mind when he wrote to Timothy, 'Do your best to present yourself to God as one approved, a workman who does not need to be ashamed and who correctly handles the word of truth' (2 Tim. 2:15).

Ezra was not only obedient to God's Word, he also rejoiced in *the fellowship of God's people.* He gives credit to the **'priests, Levites, singers, gatekeepers and temple servants'**, who **'came up to Jerusalem'** (7:7) with him; he was not a loner but part of a team that served the Lord together. This group of like-minded people encouraged Ezra on the arduous journey and later in the reforms which he initiated. The book of Ezra is not just about one man, but about all of God's people working as one to construct the temple and, more importantly, to build again the nation on the foundation of God's Word. Christians are members of Christ's body, in which every member needs every other member for the church to be a healthy and functioning body (1 Cor. 12). The isolated Christian is an unbiblical Christian!

Ezra's authority (7:11-26)

Ezra set out for Jerusalem with the backing of the Persian monarch, Artaxerxes, who appointed him 'Secretary of State for Jewish Affairs'[4] in Judah. The king's letter to Ezra demonstrates once more that the sovereign God has power to sway even the heart of a heathen monarch for the benefit of his own people. Artaxerxes' claim to be **'king of kings'** (7:12) was empty boasting which could not impede the will of the almighty God. Artaxerxes' letter, written in Aramaic, the official language of Persia, authorized Ezra, 'accompanied by any of his people who so wished (13), to go to Jerusalem to ensure the proper observance of the divine law (14,25ff.). It also dealt with two matters of supply: first, a grant towards the cost of sacrifices (15-18), and an issue of Temple vessels (19); secondly, an order to the provincial treasurers, empowering Ezra to claim certain extra supplies (21-23), also exempting Temple officials of every grade from tax (24). Its final paragraph (25f.) called on Ezra to set up a judicial system with full powers of punishment, but also to see that the people were not left in ignorance of the law.'[5] Artaxerxes trusted Ezra so much that he was prepared to make him responsible not only for the divine law but also for the civil law (7:25-26).

Ezra's acknowledgement (7:27-28)

In these two verses the text reverts back to the Hebrew. They also begin the section, which runs through to 9:15, in which Ezra writes in the first person. Ezra ascribes every blessing to God's power and goodness towards him and his fellow-Jews. It was God who **'put it into the king's heart'** to provide support for the temple in Jerusalem (7:27) and gave Ezra **'good favour'** with the king and his advisers (7:28). The word 'favour' is translated as 'steadfast love' in the Amplified Bible; the Hebrew word is related to the Old Testament word for 'stork', 'a bird known for its affection and devotion to its young'.[6] God had expressed his love for his covenant people in ordering the political situation so that they could return to Judah, but the purpose of God was more comprehensive than the Jews' return from exile: it also embraced the salvation of God's elect drawn from all the races of the world.

In verse 28 Ezra recalls that the sight of Artaxerxes' **'advisers and all the king's powerful officials'** did not

intimidate him because **'the hand of the Lord'** gave him
courage as he called together the leaders of Israel to brief them
for the journey home. The words, **'I took courage,'** indicate
that he derived his strength from the Lord, just as the apostle
Paul was to do later when facing the threat of execution in a
Roman prison: 'I can do everything through him who gives me
strength' (Phil. 4:13). Ezra would need all the resources of
God to actually get the Jews on the move to Judah, 'for a
powerful signature is sometimes easier to get, and to give, than
the volunteers to take advantage of it'.[7]

9.
The perilous journey

Please read Ezra chapter 8

To travel just under a thousand miles in four months was an amazing accomplishment for Ezra and the Jewish exiles. It is hard for us in the age of supersonic flight — *Concorde* can fly 3,553 miles in less than three hours — to appreciate the difficulties encountered in that exhausting and dangerous trek back to Judah. The journey of the immigrants began on 1 Nisan (March/April) in the seventh year of King Artaxerxes, and was completed on 1 Ab (July/August) 458 B.C. (7:7-9). The exiles returned home in fulfilment of the promise made to Jeremiah (Jer. 29:10), to the land given by God to Abraham and his posterity (Gen. 15:7,17-21). The 'seed' (AV, translated as 'offspring' in the NIV) of whom God spoke to Abraham and through whom blessing would come to the whole world was the Lord Jesus Christ (Gen. 12:7; 13:15-16; 24:7; Gal. 3:16-18). The Jews' migration back to the promised land was an essential part of the unfolding drama of redemption.

The journey begins (8:1-14)

When we compare Ezra 2:3-35 with 8:1-14 we discover that in every case, with the exception of Joab (8:9), the families of Ezra's day were the relatives of those who had returned eighty years before. The number of families was smaller and the members of each family less numerous. At the time of the first return 49,897 (2:64-65) travelled home, whereas at the second return only 1,496 adult males made the journey to Judah (8:1-14), plus the thirty-eight Levites and the 220 temple servants (8:18-20), a total of 1,754 males. Of course, many of these men were married with children (8:21), though no one bothered to count the wives and children; therefore the overall figure for the exiles varies among the commentaries between 5,000[1] and 7,000[2]. The truth of the matter is that we do not know the precise number of Jews who accompanied Ezra on his trip to Judah. There is a peculiar expression in verse 13, **'the last ones'**, which has been interpreted in various ways; it probably means that the whole family of Adonikam had settled in Judah.

Why were there fewer families returning with Ezra than with Zerubbabel? To reply that there were less people to return does not take into account the spiritual declension hidden below the surface. Coleman Luck suggests two reasons: 'There is a strong adventurous appeal to the idea of being for the first time released from captivity and going back to an almost unknown motherland to do strictly pioneer work. But when Ezra made his journey the project was no longer novel because there had been Jews in Palestine for many years. And in addition the work in Judea was in a depressed and discouraging condition. These factors certainly made the romantic appeal practically nil.'[3] When a church is planted, or some Christian enterprise established, there should be high ideals and clearly defined objectives, accompanied by unbounded enthusiasm to get the venture off the drawing-board. However, it is not so easy to keep that vision alive when the work becomes disheartening and the original pioneers have gone to heaven!

It is characteristic of a man who knew the value of teamwork to enumerate those who wended their way to Judah at his side. Similarly, the local church will not progress without co-operation between members. It is the responsibility of church leaders to lead the church by delegating tasks so as to encourage every member to participate in the Lord's work. Idle members soon degenerate into disgruntled members!

Ezra directed his appeal to the heads of the families, knowing that in most cases they would bring their families with them (8:1). Has our evangelism been directed too much to individuals and to segments of society (e.g., children or women) instead of being family-orientated? Have we paid enough attention to reaching men with the gospel? We ought to pray for the conversion of whole families. Ezra gathered families together, including children, to hear the reading and exposition of the 'Book of the Law' (Neh. 8:2-3).

A pause for reflection (8:15)

On the ninth day after departing from Babylon the returning exiles paused for three days **'at the canal that flows towards Ahava'**. The exact site of Ahava is unknown but the canal was probably a tributary of the Euphrates, and an important departure-point for the caravans travelling west. This halt was not a waste of precious time but provided space for Ezra to take stock of their situation. It is wise for Christians and churches to assess the work undertaken for the Lord. Here is a check-list to think about:

> Is my service effective?
> What am I achieving?
> What goals do I need to set myself?
> Am I frittering away time and burning up energy on unnecessary tasks?
> If I am a pastor/church officer, am I motivating others to labour for the Saviour?

As a church member am I fully committed to the Lord's work?

Pastors should delegate some of their work so that others gain experience in Christian service and they are released to open up new ministries.

God's man for the hour (8:15-31)

Verses 15-31, which record the results of Ezra's three-day stocktaking at the canal, also give us an insight into the character of this remarkable man. Ezra displayed five traits which equipped him to be God's man for the hour.

1. His wisdom (8:16-20)

Ezra surveyed the families who had journeyed so far in his company and realized that no one from the tribe of Levi was represented, nor their aides, **'the temple servants'** (8:20). These temple officials, who assisted the Levites, while not actually priests, performed essential duties without which the worship and sacrifices could not run efficiently. We should not despise the army of unsung and unpaid workers, often women, who plod on behind the scenes attending to many mundane chores.

Why were there so few of the Levites who should have been at the forefront of the people returning to Judah? 'It was only natural for these men to shrink from a prospect which was doubly daunting: not only the uprooting which all the pilgrims faced, but the drastic change from ordinary pursuits to the strict routines of the Temple.'⁴ Many of them were not prepared for this radical upheaval. There are believers, like the Levites, who show lamentable lack of commitment to the Lord's work in the church. Some put their homes, careers, hobbies and recreations before spiritual activities; the cause of God is low down on the list of their priorities. Why is it that they feel that it is expecting too much for them after a day's work to get involved in serving the Saviour who poured out his blood to redeem them from the torments of hell?

It was Ezra's responsibility as leader of God's pilgrim people to initiate the search for Levites and temple servants, just as it is the undertaking of church officers to discern areas of deficiency in the church and to seek the workers to rectify the situation. So Ezra selected nine men respected as **'leaders'** in the community, plus two men, **'Joiarib and Elnathan'**, renowned as **'men of learning'** (8:16); presumably this means that they were skilled in their understanding of God's law and could therefore persuade the Levites of their duty towards God and his people and thus urge them to travel with Ezra to Judah. Ezra sent these men, with explicit instructions about what they were to say, to a man named **'Iddo'** who is described as **'the leader in Casiphia'** (8:17). We are given no further information about either Iddo or the location of Casiphia. Evidently there was a sizeable Jewish community in Casiphia, including Levites and temple servants, under the oversight of Iddo. The outcome of this judicious arrangement was that thirty-eight Levites, along with no less than 220 temple assistants, joined those who returned (8:18-20).

2. His piety (8:21,23)

Ezra **'proclaimed a fast'** (8:21), as an acknowledgement of his sinfulness and as an expression of his serious desire to know divine guidance and protection. He asked God to be the guardian of his people: **'We ... humble ourselves before our God and ask him for a safe journey for us and our children, with all our possessions'** (8:21). The mention of 'our children' is a plea from the tender-hearted Ezra to the compassionate heart of the loving heavenly Father. Parents may beseech God the Father for the physical and spiritual safety of their children. Nor did Ezra think it selfish to pray for the safekeeping of their possessions, the loss of which would cause stress to the Jews who had given up so much to obey the Lord (8:21).

In verse 23 Ezra tells us about his prayer to God at the Ahava Canal: **'So we fasted and petitioned our God.'** The word 'petitioned' reveals the intensity of the praying, providing us with an example of 'the prayer of a righteous man' which is 'powerful and effective' (James 5:16). This is the kind of praying God longs to hear before he grants conversions and revival! Ezra's prayer, presented on behalf of Israel, flows out of their special relationship with the covenant God. He was 'our God'; therefore **'He answered our prayer.'** How slow we are to pray when God is so willing to answer our supplications!

3. His faith (8:22-23)

Ezra had originally used very strong terms in telling King Artaxerxes that Jehovah was a powerful God who would surely protect those who trusted and obeyed him: **'We had told the king, "The gracious hand of our God is on everyone who looks to him..."'** Now with the journey imminent he began to realize acutely the hazards they would face. Ezra did not feel that he could request assistance from the king because in his estimation the reputation of God himself was at stake. Artaxerxes, who later gave Nehemiah a military escort when he travelled to Judah (Neh. 2:7-9), would willingly have provided protection for Ezra. Kidner comments that Ezra's refusal of a guard and Nehemiah's acceptance of it were both 'attitudes of faith, and each in its different way (like the options of Rom.14:6) gave acceptable honour to God'.[5] We ought not to be too quick to judge other believers.

Ezra's faith in God was now put to the test. Prayer and fasting were the weapons of his warfare (8:23). It may have seemed irresponsible for Ezra not to seek the custody of the monarch for such a vast company of people, especially as women and children were among the travellers. But for Ezra it was inconsistent that he should solicit a band of pagan soldiers to defend God's people and the treasures of God's temple. He wanted God alone to receive praise for the safe arrival of his own people. His confidence in God was rewarded (8:31-32). The church is not to depend on the wealth and patronage of the ungodly. To the unbeliever dominated by the outlook of this world faith may look like foolishness but God never fails those who trust in him.

4. His prudence (8:24-30)

I like the down-to-earth shrewdness of Ezra! Faith and prudence are not incompatible. The treasure was of enormous value, and as it belonged to the Lord all of it had to be accounted for. Ezra weighed out 650 talents of silver (22 metric tons), 100 talents of silver and gold articles (3.4 metric tons of each metal), twenty golden bowls valued at 1,000 darics (about 8.5 kilograms, 8:26-27). To transport treasure of this value today would require a strong guard of men with an armoured car, yet the Jews conveyed it over 900 miles through country infested with **'enemies and bandits'** (8:31). There was the risk that some of the priests might pilfer some of this treasure for themselves, even as Achan had stolen that which was consecrated to the Lord (Josh. 7). Our handling of money belonging to the Lord or to Christian organizations needs to be dealt with in a businesslike manner so that everything is seen to be 'above board'. We ought to note the words of verse 28: **'You as well as these articles are consecrated to the Lord.'** The term 'consecrated' means 'set aside for the use of God'.

Once we belong to God then all that we possess belongs to him too.

5. His gratitude to God (8:31)

Ezra's wisdom, piety, faith and prudence were useless without God's might to preserve the migrating Jews. Ezra acknowledges that it was God who kept them safe through the long, perilous haul to Jerusalem: **'The hand of our God was on us, and he protected us from enemies and bandits along the way.'** Are we quick to thank God for his goodness to us?

Arrival in Jerusalem (8:32-36)

Four months later Ezra and the people of God arrived in Jerusalem. After a well-earned three-day rest the Jews accounted for the treasure (8:33-34) and offered sacrifices to the Lord (8:35). **'The king's orders'** (8:36) authorized Ezra to enforce the Jewish law throughout the province. The **'royal satraps'** pledged their support **'to the people and to the house of God'** (8:36). The Persian empire was made up of twenty-eight states known as satrapies. The title 'satrap' was derived from an old Persian word meaning 'protector of the realm'. Ezra 8 records 'much planning and preparation (1-36a), and little of the main work (36b). It is often in the planning stages that battles are won and by their modesty that great men are recognized.'[6] Ezra had accomplished an outstanding feat in bringing the Jewish exiles back to Jerusalem. Sadly this sense of satisfaction was short-lived. Soon he was to be faced with the greatest moral and religious crisis of the restoration era.

10.
How to pray

Please read Ezra chapter 9

It is not long after conversion that the new Christian realizes that prayer is hard work and that it is not always easy in the rush of life to find time to pray. The value of a chapter such as Ezra 9 is that it teaches us how to shape our own prayers and underlines for us the importance of prayer in our individual lives and the corporate life of the church. Ezra and Nehemiah (see Neh. 1) let us listen in as they petition God. They are not parading their spirituality but rather teaching us how to pray. My brother-in-law got hooked on golf, so to improve his game he bought himself a video machine so that he could spend all his spare moments watching Nick Faldo play. His golf improved considerably! Ezra 9 may be compared to a prayer video instructing us how to beseech our heavenly Father.

Ezra knew how to pray in times of crisis because he was familiar with the path to the throne of grace. He was on 'speaking terms with God' at all times. The major motif of Ezra's prayer is confession. The condition of the nation (9:1-4) prompted his heartfelt confession to God (9:5-15). The failure of Christians and the wickedness of unbelievers should result not in paralysing despair but in earnest supplication to the almighty God.

The condition of the Jews (9:1-4)

Four months after Ezra's arrival in Jerusalem (7:9; 10:8-9) the leaders of Judah reported to him that some of the Jews, God's own people, were marrying their non-Jewish, idol-worshipping neighbours. 'One can imagine the awful disappointment, the poignant grief'[1] of Ezra when this situation was revealed to him. They were on the verge of repeating the circumstances that had led to the exile. It is not clear why Ezra was unaware of these hybrid marriages, or, if he was aware of them, why he had not acted sooner to rectify the abuses. One possible solution to this problem is that he travelled extensively to establish his credentials to the officials of the Persian empire, in which case the opening words of Ezra 9, **'After these things had been done,'** refer back to 8:36.

Why did the leaders bring news of these marriages to Ezra? They were not meddling gossips but men whose concern was born as a result of the applicatory preaching of Ezra (7:10). They not only heard his expositions but were determined to implement the teaching received. Their consciences had been so aroused that they resolved that something had to be done about this sad defection. They did not try to excuse the people, or hush up this situation; rather they took the obligations of leadership seriously and therefore placed the facts before Ezra, expecting immediate attention. There are occasions when those in civil or spiritual authority have to enforce unpleasant policies for the benefit of the community or the church. Civil and spiritual officials are not to flinch from their duty, but to remember that they are ultimately answerable to God, the Judge of all the earth. Pleasing God is more important than pleasing people. Ezra, once informed, lost no time in setting reformation in motion. He was so zealous that he needed to be cautioned to handle the complex state of affairs more slowly! (10:12-14). When God, through the reading or preaching of the Bible, points the finger at sin in our lives, or some deficiency in our churches, then we must repent and do our utmost to make amends.

The end of verse 1 gives a list of the nations into which the Jews had married at various times in their history. At the time of Ezra **'the Canaanites'** lived around Tyre and Sidon; **'the Hittites'** were two tribes who once resided in Southern Palestine and Syria; **'the Perizzites'** and **'Jebusites'** formerly made their homes in the hills of Judea; the **'Ammonites'** and the **'Moabites'** were descendants of the daughters of Lot and the **'Amorites'** were mostly wandering shepherds who originated from Syria. In addition to these races Ezra mentions the **'Egyptians'**. Some of these nations (e.g. Hittites, Perizzites) did not exist any more. The ancient Jews were not allowed to marry into pagan races, such as the Hittites, so Ezra's contemporaries were barred from marrying into heathen nations, such as the Ammonites and Moabites.[2] The nations named were those which God had commanded the Jews, in the days of Joshua, to destroy utterly as the executioners of his wrath against their sins. His orders were never fully obeyed and the Jews of Ezra's period reaped the consequences of a former generation's disobedience. Decisions made now as individuals and as churches will influence the lives of those yet unborn. 'Old sins cast long shadows' would be an apt title for verse 1.

Marriages to Canaanites were explicitly forbidden by God through his servant Moses at the time when the Jews were on the edge of the promised land (Deut. 7:2-6). The offenders could not plead ignorance as an excuse for their actions. Though the Jews had left Babylon their hearts remained in that foreign city. In verse 2 Ezra clearly explains why these cross-racial marriages were banned: **'They ... have mingled the holy race with the peoples around them.'** These words look back to the chapter in Deuteronomy already alluded to, in which God speaks of his unique relationship with his people: 'You are a people holy to the Lord your God. The Lord your God has chosen you out of all the peoples on the face of the earth to be his people, his treasured possession. The Lord did not set his affection on you and choose you because you were more numerous than other peoples, for you were the fewest of all peoples. But it was because the Lord loved you...' (Deut. 7:6-8). Ezra 9 is teaching us that those who belong to the holy God are to be holy in their conduct. To be holy means that whatever the cost, we do not compromise in any way with the ungodly. We are not ashamed to be known as Christians in whatever company we are found.

How does the teaching of Ezra 9 work out in practice? Let me suggest some examples.

Firstly, believers are not to marry unbelievers (1 Cor. 7:39; 2 Cor. 6:14). The Christian married to a non-Christian puts himself/herself in a position where it is difficult to live wholly by the principles of the Bible. The believer with an unconverted spouse is often not free to attend services, or able to be fully committed to the Lord's work. There may be conflict about the discipline of the children, especially over issues such as the kind of television programmes the children are allowed to watch and if the television is to be used on a Sunday.

Secondly, churches are not to co-operate in evangelism or join together in acts of worship with those who deny the gospel. Heretical teachers should not be tolerated in our pulpits, or students encouraged to attend theological colleges where such men teach. The god they propound is a figment of their own imaginations rather than the God who reveals himself in the Bible (look up the strong language used by Paul and John in Galatians 1:8-9 and 2 John 10-11).

When Ezra heard about the hybrid marriages he behaved like a demented person, tearing his cloak and pulling hair out of his head and beard (9:3). The tearing of garments was an oriental mode of expressing grief that is frequently found in the Bible (e.g. Josh. 7:6; Job 1:20). Pulling out hair from the head and beard was an unusual token of distress. Ezra's dismay may seem rather melodramatic to us in an age when marriages between people of different cultures are now acceptable. When I lived in the East End of London it was commonplace to see a black man with a white partner, or vice-versa. Was Ezra's response over the top? He was not a racist, but he knew that these marriages would result in the Jews adopting the gods of their idol-worshipping wives. His trauma was that of one who has made God's cause his own. He was concerned that the Jews would abandon God and take up the **'detestable practices'** (9:11) of these depraved nations. It is clearly stated in Deuteronomy 18:9-13 that these 'detestable practices' included child sacrifices connected with the rituals of witchcraft. Ezra's attitude was mild compared with that of Nehemiah who some years later pulled out the hair of the Jewish men who married the idolaters! (Neh. 13:25). Ezra was speechless and stunned that after all the sufferings of Israel they should start on a downward course away from the Lord. His reaction stands in stark contrast to the laid-back religion of the last decade of the twentieth century.

As Ezra sat for several days mourning the sinfulness of the nation, he was joined by **'everyone who trembled at the words of the God of Israel ... because of this unfaithfulness of the exiles'** (9:4). Israel had behaved like an unfaithful wife; therefore they shook lest God should punish his people again. Do the sins of Christians move us to tears? We can become so accustomed to ungodliness that it no longer appals us. We are to weep for those who will not weep for themselves. The revival we long for will only come when we experience something of Ezra's grief and astonishment.

The confession of Ezra (9:5-15)

Ezra's prayer was the outpouring of a broken heart before a gracious God. He fell on his knees and spread his hands out to the Lord as an indication of his dependence on God. This prayer of confession was offered to God at the time of **'the evening sacrifice'** (9:5), which was between 2.30 and 3.30 p.m. It had become the custom for the Jews to gather at that time each day for prayer in one of the temple courts. It was as the sweet fragrance of the sacrifice reached Ezra's nostrils that he was delivered from his speechless anguish and poured out his soul in confession to the Lord. The sacrifice of Christ the Lamb of God is the only basis on which we may plead with God to pardon our sins. The blood of Christ gives us confidence to approach God.

There are three aspects of this prayer which blend together.

1. Identification

Ezra confessed the sins of the nation as his own: **'Our sins are higher than our heads and our guilt has reached to the heavens. From the days of our forefathers until now, our guilt has been great. Because of our sins, we ... have been subjected to the sword...'** (9:6-7). He was more **'ashamed and disgraced'** by the national guilt than any of his fellow Jews. This feature of identification is also found in the prayer of the Levites when Ezra read from 'the Book of the Law of the Lord' (Neh. 9), and in the prayers of Daniel (Dan. 9), and Isaiah (Isa. 6). Ezra's humility is the complete opposite of the attitude of the men of Jeremiah's time who recklessly sinned but felt no shame at all:

Are they ashamed of their loathsome conduct?

No, they have no shame at all;
they do not even know how to blush

(Jer. 6:15).

Their brazen disregard of God's law reaped the seventy years
of exile in Babylon. The words of Jeremiah have a familiar
ring about them as we view the world at the present time.
Identification is the key to effective prayer. A greater than Ezra
was 'numbered with the transgressors ... he bore the sin of
many, and made intercession for the transgressors' (Isa. 53:12).
Those who know the divine Intercessor pray with tenderness
for sinners.

2. Confession

Firstly, *the sin of Judah was great* (9:6). Ezra compares the
sins of the nation to a flood which had spread across the whole
land causing devastation and chaos. The waters of wickedness
were so great that they **'reached to the heavens'** (9:6) and
they could no longer be ignored by God, who punishes sinners.

Secondly, *their sin was persistent* (9:7). The Jews were
repeating the sins of their forefathers. Sin, like a hereditary
disease, is passed from one generation to another. Children
copy their parents and then act as sinful models for their own
children, and so the endless cycle goes round and round.

Thirdly, *it was widespread* (9:1-2,7). All classes of society
had sinned, from the king on his throne down to the men and
women in the streets. Even the priests in the temple were guilty
of heinous sins which were a disgrace for those set aside for the
service of God.

Fourthly, *they were defying God* (9:10-12). The Jews had
wilfully disobeyed the law of God, which forbade marriage to
idol-worshipping spouses. Sin is rebellion against the Lord.

Fifthly, *their sin deserved punishment* (9:14-15). Past sins had been revived; therefore the nation was in danger of a repeat dose of God's wrath. 'The prayer ends with clear recognition that God has every right to wash His hands of this community, as He had once threatened to do with an earlier generation (Exod. 32:10). This was no exaggerated fancy. There were other Israelites scattered abroad, through whom the promises could be fulfilled. Ezra had not even the heart to plead, as Moses had, that God's name would suffer in such a case. His prayer was naked confession, without excuses, without the pressure of so much as a request.'[3] The merciful God did not destroy his incorrigible people, but called them to repentance through the prayer of Ezra, because of the promises he made concerning the coming of the Lord Jesus Christ.

3. Gratitude

Ezra thanks God that he has shown mercy in his righteous anger. He had delivered a remnant from Babylon and sustained that remnant for eighty years in Judah. The theme of the **'remnant'** (9:8,14,15) is one which runs throughout the Bible. Whatever happens, or however wicked the world becomes, God will always have his people who remain faithful to him and who are saved from extinction.

God gave his people **'a firm place'** in the land of Judah (9:8). A literal translation from the Hebrew of 'a firm place' would be 'a tent peg'. This may relate to the nomad who could pitch his tent only where he had a right to do so. It was God, the Creator, who gave the Jews authority to settle in the land of Judah. On the other hand, there may be a reference to the tabernacle, which was fastened with bronze tent pegs (Exod. 27:19). The temple was seen as a safe place for God's people. Another suggestion I came across in my reading is that the peg refers to the iron bolt fixed firmly in the kitchen wall to hold pots and pans. Such a peg was considered to be unmoveable. However the metaphor is understood, the point is that God, who prompted the Persian kings to release his people, was not going to abandon them now, though they deserved destruction (9:9).

The **'wall of protection'** in verse 9 is not a reference to the walls of Jerusalem, which were not built until the arrival of Nehemiah, but is a description of God, the protector of his elect. All the combined forces of hell cannot destroy the church built on Christ the Rock (Matt. 16:18; cf. Rom. 8:31).

Verse 13 is a wonderful verse! In spite of our **'great guilt'** and **'our sins'**, the God of grace does not exact the full punishment that we deserve. God granted Judah deliverance instead of annihilation. God's mercy is a spur to repentance and obedience. At this point I suggest that you pause and meditate for a moment on Psalm 103:8-14. (Better still read the whole psalm!)

The sequel to Ezra's prayer was costly and painful separation from the sinful mixed marriages (ch. 10). Our prayers are hollow words if they do not lead us to holiness!

11.
Holy people for a holy God

Please read Ezra chapter 10

Many people regard prayer as an inane and useless exercise which produces no tangible results. A letter from CARE to its supporters quoted the magazine of the National Secular Society: 'Nobody is listening: Christians who actually believe in the power of prayer are an odd lot. For the more they bow the head, bend the knee and grovel to their God, the worse he treats them.' The magazine article also claimed that the Almighty is 'masochistic' and those who pray are 'sycophantic suppliants'. The response that Lyndon Bowring (Executive Chairman of CARE) gave to this was: 'We believe unequivocally in prayer' — so did Ezra![1]

The Christian knows from experience that God does answer prayer, though at times he appears to turn a deaf ear to our supplications. Isaiah wrestled with this problem of unanswered prayer:

Surely the arm of the Lord is not too short to save,
    nor his ear too dull to hear.
But your iniquities have separated
    you from your God;
your sins have hidden his face from you

                    (Isa. 59:1-2).

Sin was separating the Jews from God in the days of Ezra. It was therefore essential that Ezra's prayer in the previous chapter should be followed up with repentance which was backed up by separation from the foreign wives.

True prayer leads to repentance (10:1-8)

It is hardly surprising that **'a large crowd of Israelites — men, women and children — gathered round'** Ezra when they saw him **'praying and confessing, weeping and throwing himself down before the house of God'** (10:1). This was strange behaviour for such an eminent person. The cause of Ezra's intense agitation was the marriage of God's people to non-Jewish, idol-worshipping wives. The tears of the people mingled with those of Ezra. The wives and children would have wept at the prospect of parting from their husbands and fathers if they had an inkling of the traumatic events about to take place. As Ezra prayed, so God was answering his servant by preparing the consciences of the guilty people. His prayer of confession paved the way for reformation.

The voice of a man named Shecaniah, a leader among the Jews, was raised above the noise of the weeping, publicly confessing the sins of Israel and demanding prompt action to deal with the situation (10:2-4). It is interesting to note that though Shecaniah's name is not on the list of men who married pagan wives (10:18-43), he nevertheless included himself among those who disobeyed the Lord: **'We have been unfaithful to our God'** (10:2). His words rescued the people from despair: **'But in spite of this, there is still hope for Israel.'** He may have based his 'hope' on the promise of Deuteronomy 30:9-10: 'The Lord will again delight in you ... if you obey the Lord your God and keep his commands ... and turn to the Lord your God with all your heart and with all your soul.' These words of Moses link forgiveness —'The Lord will ... delight in you' — with repentance —'turn to the Lord'. When we detest our sin and turn wholeheartedly from it then God will pardon us. God's infinite grace is greater than all our sins. The most hardened sinner or wayward Christian can be forgiven when there is genuine repentance.

Shecaniah proposed that a covenant (a solemn and binding promise) be made with God: **'Now let us make a covenant before our God to send away all these women and their children.'** His recommendation was a summons to obey God: **'Let it be done according to the Law'** (10:3). The treatment for the malady was such a drastic one that Shecaniah urged Ezra to exert himself at once, pledging the backing of the leaders of Judah: **'Rise up; this matter is in your hands. We will support you, so take courage and do it'** (10:4). Ezra responded to Shecaniah's appeal by compelling the Jews to swear an oath of obedience to God; then he fasted as he mourned over the transgression of God's people (10:5-6). Ezra sought solitude for prayer in the **'room of Jehohanan'**, who was presumably a priest who resided in the temple.[2] This privacy reveals to us the sincerity of Ezra's 'dramatic gestures of dismay'[3] in his public prayer in chapter 9. Our eloquent supplications in the prayer meeting are insincere if we do not pray in our homes when only God can hear us. Ezra does not condemn his countrymen, but he weeps for them when he is alone in the presence of the Lord. Do we weep over the sins of the church and the nation?

Ezra's solicitude for his fellow Jews did not stop with prayer; he issued a proclamation calling all the male Israelites to meet him in Jerusalem within three days (10:7-8). The farthest boundary was no more than forty miles away, so it would be easy for them to gather within the prescribed time. This edict was a joint one from Ezra and the leaders, though Ezra was armed with the authority of King Artaxerxes to

punish them for non-compliance (7:26). The order of the local
officials 'would carry more moral weight than imperial decrees'.⁴A penalty was placed on failure to attend: goods would
be confiscated and given to the priests, and non-attending
males would be banished from the chosen race. These severe
measures meant that the excommunicated Jew would not be
allowed to participate in the daily sacrifices for the removal of
his sins, or able to draw on the help and friendship of fellow
Jews in times of trouble. If a Jewish male did not attend it
would reveal that spiritually he did not belong to the people of
God.

True repentance leads to separation (10:9-17)

Three days later, **'All the men of Judah and Benjamin had
gathered in Jerusalem'** (10:9) in the open square in front of
the temple. It has been estimated that this square was large
enough to accommodate 20,000 men, though the number in
the assembly was probably less than that.⁵ The year was 458
B.C. and it was the ninth month, Chisleu, equivalent to our
December, in the middle of the rainy season (which usually
started around the middle of October). **'All the people were
sitting in the square before the house of God, greatly
distressed by the occasion and because of the rain.'** Verse
9 'captures for us the shivering misery of the scene'.⁶ The
company were dismal but determined to obey God's Word
whatever the cost. If the consciences of these men had been
sensitive a few years before they would have saved themselves
their present distress. Unconfessed sins, sooner or later, reap
sorrow.

Ezra's sermon was short and to the point: **'You have been
unfaithful; you have married foreign women, adding to**

Israel's guilt. Now make confession to the Lord, the God of your fathers, and do his will. Separate yourselves from the peoples around you and from your foreign wives' (10:10-11). He was faithful to God as he plainly reproved his hearers' misdemeanour, calling for confession to the Lord and commanding repentance. The required evidence of turning back to God was separation from the ungodly, especially from their idol-worshipping wives. It is no use talking about repentance unless we are prepared to break off our friendship with the world (James 4:4; 1 John 2:15-17).

The whole assembly gave a resounding 'yes' vote to the words of Ezra: **'You are right! We must do as you say'** (10:12). However, they cautioned him against undue haste (10:13). This recommendation was not to delay obedience but to allow time for the procedure to be sorted out. There was a genuine desire that sin should be abandoned and reform carried out so that God's wrath would be averted from the nation (10:14). The inclement weather (10:9,13) made some delay inevitable; therefore judges were appointed to handle the divorce cases over a longer period of time. It was proposed that the men married to foreign wives should come **'at a set time, along with the elders and judges of each town'** (10:14) to Jerusalem for investigation. The presence of the 'elders and judges' who knew the circumstances of the men would ensure that every case would be carefully and fairly scrutinized. This was so important because it was heart-rending for the families, especially for the wives, involved in the separations. It is easier to depart from God than to return to him. The bitter fruit of our defection may haunt us for the rest of our lives.

Only four men, **'Jonathan ... and Jahzeiah ... supported by Meshullam and Shabbethai, the Levite'**, protested against the divorce of the idolatrous women (10:15). These dissenters, who probably wanted to protect their relatives and friends, may have felt that the remedy for the delinquent behaviour was too harsh. The divorced wives and their children would have gone back into their extended non-Jewish families from which they came. It has been suggested that some of the Jewish men had already divorced Jewish wives in order to marry pagan women.

A. E. Cundell helps us to get the situation into perspective: 'The unhappiness caused by these broken homes must be set not only against the initial transgression involved in the contracting of the marriages, but also against the ultimate blessing to the whole world that could come only through a purified community.'[7] Israel must remain a distinct nation so that the promises relating to the coming of Messiah would be fulfilled. The advent of the Saviour hinged on the obedience of Ezra and the people of God.

The enquiry and divorce proceedings (10:16-17) took about three months, from the first day of the tenth month (Tebeth, December/January), to the first day of the first month (Nisan, March/April). We read the names of seventeen priests (10:18-22), plus a further ten Levites, among them some singers and gatekeepers (10:23-24). There are textual variations in verse 38 which determine how we calculate the number of Israelites married to non-Jewish wives (10:25-43). It is either eighty-six (as in the AV) or eighty-four (as in the NIV), which gives a total of 113 or 111, depending on which version is correct. The offenders **'all gave their hands in pledge to put away their wives, and for their guilt they each presented a ram from the flock as a guilt offering'** (10:19). As we read on into the book of Nehemiah we discover that the Jews had short memories. Nehemiah spent time dealing with the same problem of marriages between Jews and Gentiles (Neh. 13:23-27). Christians too have a tendency to lapse into old sins. The holy God demands holy people to serve him.

At this point Ezra disappears from the record until thirteen years later, when we find him expounding God's law to the

Jews (Neh. 8). Now Nehemiah moves into the limelight. We can be sure that Ezra continued to labour among God's people but he was no longer the prominent figure. His special work was done; Ezra possessed the humility and wisdom to discern that fact. The temptation when the Lord uses one of his servants is to think that he must continue in the foremost place. This brings sorrow to the man himself and failure to the people of God. The Lord who uses one person today may employ someone else tomorrow. Are we willing to be anything or nothing so long as the Lord is exalted?

Ezra entered Jerusalem in 458 B.C. with the intention of rebuilding the people of God into a people whose lives were pleasing to God. He achieved this goal by calling them back to renewed obedience to the Word of God. This obedience was costly and painful, but essential, for it opened the way to a fresh realization of the presence of God. Ezra laid the spiritual foundations on which Nehemiah was to build when he became the governor of Judah in 445 B.C.

Nehemiah

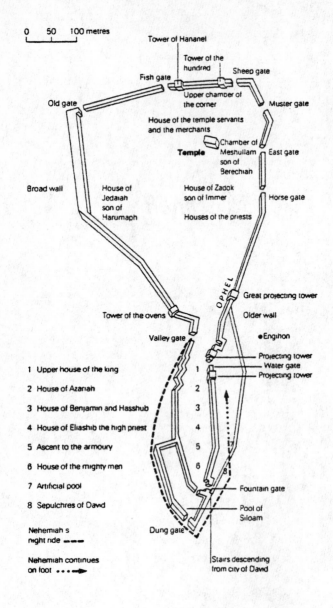

Map 2. The gates of Jerusalem.
Reproduced by courtesy of IVP.

12.
Introducing Nehemiah

There is a period of some thirteen years between the closing scene in Ezra and the prayer of Nehemiah in the first chapter of his book (compare Ezra 7:8 with Nehemiah 1:1; 2:1). The careers of Ezra the scribe and Nehemiah the governor over-lapped (12:26). An example of this is given in Nehemiah 8 where we read about them standing alongside one another at the reading of the Law at the Feast of Trumpets. Kidner draws a helpful comparison between the characters of these two men: 'Ezra was a quieter personality than the formidable, practical Nehemiah; he does not leap out of the page as this man does.'[1] The nation owed a great debt to these determined men with their different personalities and gifts.

The cupbearer

In contrast to Ezra, who gives us a list of his ancestors (Ezra 7:1-5), Nehemiah only mentions the names of his father Hacaliah and his brother Hanani (1:1,2; 7:2). Nehemiah was probably born in captivity and somehow rose to the position of cupbearer to Artaxerxes, the Persian king (1:11). As cupbearer he was an official of the royal household in a position of great influence. The cupbearer was rather like a prime minister and master of ceremonies rolled into one. In an age of intrigue and assassination the job was not without risks for the cupbearer, who tasted the wine before it was given to the king. Another responsibility of the cupbearer was to guard the sleeping quarters of the monarch.[2]

The sovereign God ordained that Nehemiah was the right man in the right place ready for his use. The whole of his life up to this point was a preparation for the rôle he was shortly to play in God's purpose for the Jews. This plan embraced the salvation of the elect from all races. Nehemiah the cupbearer 'did not forget his own people. He was prepared to forsake the luxury of a royal court and go to Jerusalem to help in the rebuilding of the city. When eventually he did go there he went as civil governor with the authority of the king of Persia.'[3] Nehemiah was a man who sought first God's kingdom and his righteousness (Matt. 6:33). This ought to be the motivation of God's people in every age.

The comforter

Nehemiah's name, which means 'Jehovah comforts', aptly sums up his ministry to the troubled Jews living among the rubble of Jerusalem, the capital city of Judah. At Nehemiah's request, the Persian king, Artaxerxes, made him governor of Judah, a post he held for twelve years (5:14; 13:6). After a time spent back in Persia he returned for a second term as governor of Judah. Nehemiah's memoirs span some fifteen years, from 445 B.C. to around 431 B.C.

'The ideal worker'

Nehemiah mentions Darius II (12:22), who reigned from 423-404 B.C. We assume therefore that Nehemiah wrote his memoirs either after his retirement or in the later years of Darius' administration. In the book of Nehemiah its author 'comes across as the ideal worker for God. The key words are prayer and work. He not only prayed and worked himself but he inspired his followers to do the same.'[4] It is a book which ought to stimulate us to supplication and service. Nehemiah chapters 1-7 are concerned with the restoration of the walls of Jerusalem and chapters 8-13 focus on the revitalizing of the people of God.

13.
Sorrow and supplication

Please read Nehemiah chapter 1

The opening verses introduce us to Nehemiah, a Jew, in the royal city of Susa, the winter residence of Artaxerxes, the Persian king. We learn from verse 11 that Nehemiah was employed as Artaxerxes' cupbearer. Judah, the homeland of Nehemiah, was a thousand miles away. However, he still retained a warm love for that land and its people. He was keenly interested in the fortunes of the descendants of the Jews who had returned to Judah almost a century earlier under the leadership of Zerubbabel, in 537 B.C., and those who had accompanied Ezra in 458 B.C.

Was this concern merely a bout of nostalgia for the 'good old days'? No! His solicitude was rooted in the conviction that the Jewish nation was chosen by God and that the land of Judah was his gift to them. The choice of the Jews and the gift of the land were part of God's plan to bring the Lord Jesus Christ into the world so that he might die for sinners on a Roman cross. Nehemiah longed to see the realization of God's promises relating to the coming of the Messiah-Saviour.

The sorrow of Nehemiah (1:1-4)

In 445 B.C., the twentieth year of Artaxerxes' reign, in the month of Kislev (November-December), Nehemiah's brother

Hanani **'came from Judah'** with sad news **'about the Jewish remnant'**. This one visit dramatically changed the course of the cupbearer's life. Indeed it was a turning-point in the history of the Jews and a further development in events which finally reached their climax in the birth of Christ. So much can hinge on something which may seem so trivial or insignificant at the time. A similar thing happened when Martin Luther nailed his ninety-five theses to the door of the Wittenberg Castle Church at midday on 31 October 1517. His protest about the selling of indulgences sparked off the Protestant Reformation.[1]

Hanani and his companions reported that the people themselves were in a disconsolate mood and the wall of Jerusalem was a heap of stones, with its gates reduced to ashes. Later Nehemiah saw for himself the destruction of Jerusalem. He then discovered that his brother had accurately reported the razing of the city (2:17). We have learnt already from the book of Ezra that all attempts to rebuild the wall (destroyed by the Babylonians in 586 B.C.) had been frustrated by 'the enemies of Judah' (Ezra 4:1,7-16). As a result very few people lived in the capital city (Neh. 11:1).

The words, **'I questioned them about the Jewish remnant that survived the exile'** (1:2) may imply that Nehemiah was already aware of the circumstances of his fellow Jews in Jerusalem, but now, 'The Holy Spirit impressed the reality of the situation upon his heart. At any rate, he was staggered, shaken to the depths of his being.'[2] The reference to 'the Jewish remnant' could be an allusion to the prophecy of Isaiah 10:20-23 relating to the return of the exiles to their homeland. Nehemiah jotted down in his diary his response to this tragic news: **'I sat down and wept. For some days I mourned and fasted and prayed before the God of heaven'** (1:4). He wept that the city and its inhabitants were defenceless. Most of all he mourned because the city which was meant to be a light to the nations had become 'an international joke' (Isa. 42:6-7; 49:6).[3] The anguish of the survivors became his own personal

sorrow. 'Since Nehemiah's natural bent was for swift, deci-
sive action, his behaviour here is remarkable. It shows where
his priorities lay. It also reveals, by every phrase in this verse
[4], the unhurried and far from superficial background to the
famous "arrow prayer" of 2:4 and to the achievements which
were to follow it.'[4]

Like the prophet Ezekiel, Nehemiah knew how to weep
with those who weep. The grief of Ezekiel was too deep for
words when he saw the plight of the exiles 'near the Kebar
river'. All he could do was sit among them 'for seven days —
overwhelmed' (Ezek. 3:15). What do we know of this em-
pathy with our fellow Christians in their suffering? The sympathy of believers for one another is beautifully expressed in
the hymn by John Fawcett:

> We share our mutual woes
> Our mutual burdens bear;
> And often for each other flows
> The sympathizing tear.[5]

We ought to weep when we consider the ineffectiveness of
so many evangelical churches to reach the unconverted
masses in our country. Our hearts should also be profoundly
disturbed at the fragmented state of evangelicalism at the
present time.

The supplication of Nehemiah (1:5-11)

Nehemiah was in Babylon and he felt powerless to help his
afflicted countrymen; therefore he turned to God in prayer. We
can discern four elements to this prayer of Nehemiah.

1. He addresses his prayer to the great and gracious God (1:5-6)

Nehemiah prays to the Lord, the **'God of heaven'**, who is superior to the most powerful kings and to all the imagined gods of the nations. He is **'great and awesome'** in his might, holiness and justice. 'The greater God becomes to him, the smaller becomes his problem.'[6] The great God is also a gracious God who **'keeps his covenant of love with those who love him and obey his commands'**. Our love and obedience do not merit his love, but are the evidence that we are indeed the objects of his grace. Nehemiah's prayer is both earnest and persistent as he pleads **'day and night'** for God's ears to be attentive and his eyes open to him. When we pray it is reassuring to realize that

> The eyes of the Lord are on the righteous
> and his ears are attentive to their cry;
> … he delivers them from all their troubles
>
> (Ps. 34:15,17).

2. He confesses his own sins and those of the nation (1:6-7)

Reflection on the character of God makes Nehemiah aware that the sorrow of the Jews is related to their sins: **'I confess the sins we … have committed against you.'** Nehemiah. like Ezra before him (Ezra 9), identifies himself with the sins of his fellow Jews. Our prayers for and help of others will be ineffective if we are like the proud, self-righteous Pharisee in the parable of Jesus. The tax collector is a better model of how to approach the Almighty. He 'stood at a distance. He would not even look up to heaven, but beat his breast and said, "God, have mercy on me, a sinner"' (Luke 18:9-14).

3. He recalls the promises of God (1:8-9)

Nehemiah calls on God to **'Remember the instruction you gave your servant Moses.'** The word 'remember' 'refers not to God's recollection of something forgotten, but to His intervention on behalf of His own'.[7] Nehemiah's reference to Moses alludes to Leviticus 26:27-45 and Deuteronomy.30:1-5. He sees God's past dealings with his people as a mirror of his future plans. The thrust of Nehemiah's reasoning may be paraphrased in the following way: 'If the *curses* were literally carried out, how much more will the promised *blessings* be fulfilled? He who is faithful in disciplining his people, which is an unpleasant task, will surely be faithful in the more delightful work of granting them favours when they obey him.' The **'farthest horizon'** to which the Jews were scattered (1:9) presented no problem to God when his time for restoration arrived. Likewise the present misery of the Jews in Judah was not beyond God's ability to bring relief to his people.

4. He appeals to God, who has a unique relationship with his people (1:10-11)

There is an emphasis in these verses on the word 'your': **'... your servants and your people, whom you redeemed ... be attentive to the prayer of this your servant and to the prayer of your servants'**. Israel belonged to God because he 'redeemed' or rescued them from bondage in Egypt. 'Most significantly in verse 10 he quotes the words in which Moses had pleaded for Israel on mount Sinai (Deut. 9:29), that God would stand by His own *(thy servants and thy people)* and by the work He had so strenuously begun. At that point Israel had been threatened with extinction; now, it seems, Nehemiah sees the situation as hardly less perilous. Like Moses, he must stand in the breach with his intercession.'[8] The salvation of sinners depended on the survival of the Jewish race. Our churches and our nation need Christians like Moses and Nehemiah who will 'stand in the breach' and supplicate God for his mercy (see Ps. 106:23).

There is another link with an earlier period of Israel's history at the beginning of verse eleven: **'O Lord, let your ear be attentive to the prayer of this your servant.'** This is similar to the petition of Solomon at the opening of the temple (2 Chron. 6:40). The prayers of both Ezra and Nehemiah reveal that their hearts were saturated with the Word of God.

When we pray we too can entreat God on the basis of his choice of us back in eternity and his purchase of us through the blood of Christ shed at Calvary. God cannot ignore such a plea! The word 'servants' (1:10,11) implies renewed submission to God. Redemption brings deliverance from sin but also demands obedience to Christ, whose precious blood was the price of our freedom (1 Cor. 6:19-20; 1 Peter 1:18-19).

The God of **'great strength'** and a **'mighty hand'** (1:10) heard the prayer of Nehemiah so that the walls of Jerusalem were restored in the remarkably short period of fifty-two days (6:15). But this accomplishment was still in the future; for the present Nehemiah was in urgent need of direction from God to know what action to take on behalf of the distressed Jews in Jerusalem. Whatever plan he formulated, he would have to speak first with King Artaxerxes. Therefore the chapter ends with Nehemiah's prayer to God for his blessing: **'Give your servant success today by granting him favour in the presence of this man'** (1:11). Nehemiah prayed for his suffering kinsmen from Kislev (November-December) 446 until Nisan (March-April) 445, a period of four months, until the opportunity arose for him to approach the king (compare 1:1 with 2:1). Do we have this same kind of commitment as we pray for other Christians?

14.
Nehemiah's new job

Please read Nehemiah chapter 2

Four months passed between Hanani's visit from Jerusalem to his brother Nehemiah (ch. 1), and the question of King Artaxerxes (ch. 2). Meanwhile Nehemiah patiently waited and prayed for guidance from God. Four months can be a long time when a Christian needs to know God's will! God's time arrived for Nehemiah in Nisan, the first month of the Jewish religious year, equivalent to our months of March/April. Now his prayers must be accompanied by vigorous activity. God has promised to lead us (Ps. 32:8), but once his will is known we must, like Nehemiah, be ready to follow!

Nehemiah's sad face (2:1-3)

Nehemiah's opportunity came unexpectedly at a banquet when he was serving wine to King Artaxerxes and Queen Damaspia (2:6).[1] The presence of the queen suggests that this was a private party. It was unusual for the queen to attend functions of a more formal nature. As the feast proceeded the king observed the downcast face of Nehemiah and discerned that the cause of his cupbearer's sadness was emotional rather than physical. A gloomy face on such an occasion was considered bad manners according to Persian rules. The Persians thought that it was impossible for anyone to be in the king's presence and not be happy! A fascinating insight into Persian etiquette is found in the book of Esther, the wife of Xerxes I (486-465 B.C.). Mordecai, her cousin, wanted to inform the queen about the suffering of her fellow Jews, but he dared not enter the palace because he was dressed in sackcloth, the symbol of mourning (Esth. 4:2). Artaxerxes overlooked Nehemiah's breach of protocol and showed genuine interest in his sorrow (2:2).

The prayer of 1:11 (note the word 'today') seems to indicate that he 'may even have decided to precipitate the enquiry by allowing his feelings to be obvious. Now the moment has come, and if he mishandles it there will not be another'.[2] Artaxerxes' wrath could result in punishment or even immediate execution. Nehemiah had good reason to be **'very much afraid'** (2:2; cf. Esth. 4:11). It was unthinkable that someone enjoying the impressive presence of the king should ask permission to go to a place miles away!

Nehemiah employs wisdom and tact as he explains his dejection. He assures Artaxerxes of his loyalty: **'May the king live for ever!'** (2:3). Throughout the Near East the tombs of the dead were regarded as sacred, therefore Nehemiah speaks of the neglected graves of his forefathers. This is an astute ploy to gain the sympathy of the monarch. Then the cupbearer mentions the destruction of Jerusalem's gates by fire, though at this stage he does not mention the actual city in question (2:3). Nehemiah was always sensitive to the feelings of other people and knew how to act accordingly — a skill so necessary for spiritual leaders within the church today.

Nehemiah's request (2:5-9)

Nehemiah's heart probably missed a beat when he heard the king's question: **'What is it you want?'** (2:4). The prayer of verse 4 has often been described as an 'arrow prayer'. Perhaps in modern parlance we might call it a 'fax prayer'. It was effective because it arose out of Nehemiah's ongoing life of prayer. It reached heaven the moment it was prayed and was answered instantaneously. We often major on the 'various hindrances we meet in coming to the mercy-seat',[3] so that we forget the promise of God concerning speedy answers to prayer: 'Before they call I will answer; while they are still speaking I will hear' (Isa. 65:24).

Nehemiah's 'fax prayer' is one of eight brief petitions recorded in his memoir (4:4-5; 5:19; 6:9,14; 13:14,22,29). It has been said that Nehemiah 'walked with God because he talked with God'.[4] Nehemiah was given courage and sagacity to reply to the king. God can give us the same boldness and prudence when suddenly faced with some awkward question or difficult situation. We may depend on the Holy Spirit to come alongside us when we are talking about the Saviour to unbelievers who may be critical and cynical. It is as we pray to the **'God of heaven'** (2:4) that we overcome our fear (2:2) and are filled with God's peace and power.

The cupbearer's request, **'Send me to the city in Judah ... so that I can rebuild it'** (2:5), required the king to do a 'U-turn' and rescind a previous edict relating to the walls of Jerusalem. The Artaxerxes of Nehemiah 2 is the same king to whom the Samaritan Rehum had sent a letter about the 'rebellious city' of Jerusalem which was 'troublesome to kings and provinces, a place of rebellion from ancient times'. Artaxerxes' response to that letter was to issue an order that 'This city will not be rebuilt until I so order' (Ezra 4:15,21). Artaxerxes could have interpreted Nehemiah's suspicious request as a plot to instigate a revolt against him. Instead he overturns his previous ruling in favour of his servant. The words, 'until I so order' (Ezra 4:21), provided the king with a convenient loophole for him to grant Nehemiah his heart's desire.

It was only the almighty God of heaven who could cause this autocratic king of Persia to change his former law for the benefit of Nehemiah and the remnant in Judah. God orders all things for the good of his people and the glory of his own name. God had in mind the future birth of his Son into a Jewish family so that he might die on a Roman cross for the salvation of his elect. The 'U-turn' of King Artaxerxes was one more link in the chain of the unfolding decrees of the all-powerful God.

Once Artaxerxes understood Nehemiah's petition he asked a second question: **'How long will your journey take, and when will you get back?'** Nehemiah responded by setting a time (2:6). 'The time set for his return will hardly have been the twelve years mentioned in 5:14 and 13:6. He is more likely to have reported back after the dedication of the walls, within the year, and then to have had his appointment as governor renewed.'⁵ Artaxerxes would be inconvenienced by the absence of his cupbearer; therefore Nehemiah was careful to preserve the king's superiority: **'If it pleases the king...'** (2:7). He was always respectful and courteous towards his sovereign.

After the king had agreed to release him from his duties as cupbearer, Nehemiah asked for letters to ensure safe-conduct while travelling to Judah (2:7), and further letters so that he could obtain timber for building (2:8). **'The citadel'** (2:8), which was on the north side of Jerusalem, served to protect both the city and the temple. The commander of this citadel was Hananiah, whom Nehemiah later appointed as one of the rulers of the repopulated Jerusalem (7:2). No doubt his brother Hanani had told Nehemiah that one of Artaxerxes' forests was near Jerusalem and was supervised by a man named Asaph (2:8). Nehemiah had done his homework well. We dissipate our energy and squander our time when we are lazy and careless in our service for the Lord. God's work demands our very best efforts (Eccl. 9:10).

Why was Artaxerxes willing to let Nehemiah go to Judah? The political situation at that time may have worked in Nehemiah's favour. The viceroy of Syria, a man by the name of Megabyrus, led a revolt against Artaxerxes. He was forced into submission but still retained his position in Syria. It was to Artaxerxes' advantage to have a loyal governor in Judah, which lay between Syria and Egypt. Nehemiah's presence in Judah made alliances between Syria and Egypt more difficult.[6] Artaxerxes not only sent Nehemiah to Jerusalem with letters, but he also gave him **'army officers and cavalry'** for defence (2:9; cf. Ezra 8:21-23).

Later, when Nehemiah recalled his interview with Artaxerxes, he praised God for his success: **'And because the gracious hand of my God was upon me, the king granted my request'** (2:8). As we have already seen, the reference to the gracious hand of God is a refrain heard several times in both the books of Ezra and Nehemiah (Ezra 7:6,9,28; 8:18; Neh. 2:18). Nehemiah realized that there is a King in heaven far greater than any earthly potentate. He feared neither the king's anger nor the displeasure of Sanballat and Tobiah (2:10).

When God blesses our service, do we congratulate ourselves, or ascribe praise to him? The temptation to pride is never far away from the Christian worker. An example of this is found in the journal of Robert Murray M'Cheyne, a Scots minister of the nineteenth century who was greatly used by God and experienced revival during his ministry at Kilsyth. His entry for 14 November 1833 reads, 'I fear the love of applause... May God keep me from preaching myself instead of Christ crucified.'[7]

Nehemiah's arrival in Jerusalem (2:11-16)

Nehemiah, who formerly worked under the supervision of King Artaxerxes, was now on his own as governor of Judah.

He left the security of the palace for the hardships of governing a disheartened nation. We read little about the actual journey of Nehemiah from Persia to Judah, in contrast to that made by Ezra (Ezra 8). Nehemiah's impressive arrival made the point to the other governors that he came into Judah with the authority of Artaxerxes the Persian king (2:9).

We assume that his first three days in Jerusalem were not spent in idleness, but were used for devising his strategy and supplicating God for strength and wisdom to fulfil his new rôle (2:11). Nehemiah, like Ezra, discovered that time devoted to prayer and planning is not wasted time (Ezra 8:15,21). Are we too busy with 'Christian service', so that we do not have time to listen to God?

On the fourth day Nehemiah **'set out during the night with a few men'** (2:12) to examine for himself the devastation of the city walls and gates. His survey confirmed all that his brother Hanani had reported to him (1:2-3). Nehemiah 'does not rush into action (11) or talk (12). He anticipates the obvious objection that a newcomer can have no idea of the task, so he briefs himself thoroughly and chooses his moment to show his hand (16)'.[8] Presumably this reconnaissance of the walls was made under cover of darkness to prevent leakage of information to his adversaries. Nehemiah wanted to formulate his strategy before he announced it to his fellow Jews and news of it reached the ears of his antagonists.

Nehemiah's call to the people (2:17-18)

Nehemiah's call to the inhabitants of Jerusalem was: **'Come, let us rebuild the wall of Jerusalem, and we will no longer be in disgrace'** (2:17). He associates himself fully with them in their distress: **'You see the trouble we are in ... let us rebuild ... we will no longer be in disgrace.'** The caring attitude of Nehemiah was in stark contrast to the selfishness of previous governors (5:14-18). His genuine concern for them inspires confidence in his leadership. Nehemiah turns the thoughts of the people away from 'trouble' and 'disgrace' (2:17) to **'the gracious hand of my God upon me'**. It was God's hand on Nehemiah which led to **'what the king had said to me'** (2:18).

The response of the Jews to Nehemiah's summons was enthusiastic: **'Let us start rebuilding.'** Their eager words were immediately followed by performance: **'So they began this good work'** (2:18). Our good resolutions must be followed by actual deeds. Nehemiah had everything ready so that they could start work at once. For ninety years the people had been too discouraged and downtrodden to attempt anything, but now they were eager to get started without any delay on the building of the walls. 'So total a response from such a group was as miraculous as that of Artaxerxes.'[9] No wonder that the assignment was completed in fifty-two days! (6:15). Oh, for Christians with this kind of 'get-up-and-go' for the Lord!

Nehemiah's enemies (2:10,19-20)

Not everyone was pleased when Nehemiah came on the scene! The enemies of the Jews in Samaria soon learnt about the appearance of a new governor in Jerusalem (2:10). Nehemiah points the finger directly at the three leading protagonists.

The first of these men was *Sanballat* (2:10), the governor of Samaria who came from Beth-Horon ('house of the god Horon'). He was a descendant of the mixed race that settled in Samaria after the Assyrian conquest (2 Kings 17:24,29-31).

Secondly, there was *Tobiah* (2:10), an Ammonite official who was from an old and famous family that ruled Ammon for years. The land of Ammon, on the east side of the Dead Sea, was inhabited by the descendants of Ben-Ammi, the son of Lot by his younger daughter (Gen. 19:30-38). Both Sanballat and Tobiah were related to the high priest in Jerusalem (13:4,5,28).

The third name in this wicked trio was *Geshem the Arab* (2:19), who was even more influential and formidable than Sanballat and Tobiah.

When the ridicule of these three men rang in Nehemiah's ears (2:19), Judah was surrounded with hostile Samaria in the north, Moab and Ammon in the east and Edom in the south. Moab and Edom were ruled by Geshem and his league of Arabian tribes. We shall read more about these three evil men as we go further on into the book of Nehemiah.

'Are you rebelling against the king?' (2:19). Such an insinuation had been sufficient on a previous occasion to halt work on the walls (Ezra 4:12-16). This time the insults did not affect the Jews because King Artaxerxes had sanctioned the project and because of their more settled confidence in the Lord: **'The God of heaven will give us success'** (2:20). It was God who had entrusted to the Jews, his servants, the work of rebuilding the walls of Jerusalem. Therefore the Samaritans who did not belong to God, and hence had no claim on the city, were not allowed to distract them from the building enterprise. The Samaritans were worried about the authority of the Persian king, but the Jews were commissioned by a King greater than the mighty Artaxerxes.

But why should 'the God of heaven' be so concerned about the crumbling walls of a Jewish city? Does he not have more essential things to occupy his mind? The safety of Jerusalem was bound up with the future of the Jewish race and the birth of Jesus Christ, 'the Saviour of the world'.

We too, like Nehemiah and the citizens of Jerusalem, are called to build. But we are not erecting a physical city, but the church, 'the city of God' (Ps. 46:4; Heb. 12:22-24). We do not build with bricks and cement, but with the tools of fervent prayer, powerful preaching and zealous personal witnessing to those who do not know the Saviour. We shall encounter opposition, but the 'God of heaven' who gave success to Nehemiah is our God!

15.
Sharing the workload

Please read Nehemiah chapter 3

Another list of people, plus all the gate-names in the city of Jerusalem! However, Nehemiah's memoir would be incomplete without this chapter which gives us an insight into the secret of his success. There are three reasons why Nehemiah accomplished so much in a short space of time. Firstly, he made a complex operation relatively simple by dividing the wall into about forty different sections. Secondly, he had the knack of getting each individual builder to labour enthusiastically and harmoniously with his fellow workers. Thirdly, and more importantly, the erection of the walls was a demonstration of God's power, which enabled the Jews to press on with their task in the face of many discouragements and hostile opposition. We may learn from Nehemiah 3 how we ought to proceed in the building of the city of God's church.

Nehemiah 3 is structured around the nine gates of Jerusalem. The account proceeds anticlockwise, starting and finishing at the Sheep Gate (3:1,32), which was near the north-eastern corner of Jerusalem. 'It has been said that this one chapter contains a greater amount of information concerning the topography of ancient Jerusalem than do all other passages put together.'[1]

The references to **'Meremoth, son of Uriah'** (3:4) and **'Malkijah, son of Harim'** (3:11) provide links between the

Doing a great work

missions of Ezra and Nehemiah. 'In Ezra 8:33 Meremoth, son
of Uriah, checked in the treasure brought by Ezra from
Babylon; and in Ezra 10:31, Malchijah, [AV spelling] son of
Harim, was one of those who submitted to Ezra's purge of
mixed marriages.'[2] The tone of the enterprise was set as
Eliashib the high priest and his colleagues dedicated the
portion of the wall which they rebuilt near the temple (3:1).
Perhaps this 'mini-dedication' service was equivalent to a sort
of foundation-stone-laying ceremony when work is started on
some new public building. Later the entire wall was consecrated with a procession and praise (12:27-43). It is impossible
to give the exact locations of **'the Tower of the Hundred'** and
'the Tower of Hananel', which were somewhere in the
vicinity of the Sheep Gate in the north of Jerusalem (3:1).
Further on in the chapter we read of another tower, **'the Tower
of the Ovens'** (3:11), which was probably near the Valley
Gate, and was presumably the site of the bakers.

Co-ordination

There are certain expressions used by Nehemiah over and over
again which may serve as a key enabling us to enter into the
spiritual principles of this chapter.

For example, such phrases as **'next to him'** (3:4 [twice],
10,17,18,19,20,21,22,24,25,29,30,31), **'next to them'**
(3:2,7,27,29,30), **'beyond him'** (3:16), **'beyond them'** (3:23)
and **'beside him'** (3:17) are used over twenty times in all. Each
man and every group had a definite place of work assigned to
them. Each person knew where he belonged and what was
expected of him. Some labourers had to rebuild their section
of the wall from scratch; others only needed to make repairs.

Another set of recurring phrases are **'in front of their
house'** (3:23), **'each in front of his own house'** (3:28),

'opposite his house' (3:29), 'opposite his living quarters' (3:30) and 'beside his house' (3:23). The builders did not waste valuable time commuting from one end of Jerusalem to the other. This practical arrangement meant that it was easy for the workers to be fed and also that in the event of attack each man was at hand to protect his own family. Thus each person was relieved from undue anxiety and pressure and was free to give of his best to the task appointed to him by Nehemiah.

The way to make progress in the building of God's city is for every worker to know precisely the undertaking assigned to him by the church officers and other church members. It is beneficial if each labourer sets himself goals towards which he strives rather than working without any clear direction. Spiritual leaders ought to anticipate potential problems and diffuse any possible causes of disunity, so that every member can channel all his efforts into the ministry of the local church.

We read three times in this chapter that Nehemiah delegated responsibility for a segment of the wall to supervisors. An example of this in found in verse 7: **'Repairs were made by men ... under the authority of the governor of the Trans-Euphrates'** (cf. 3:17-18). Day-to-day problems were sorted out by these foremen. In this way the labour force was kept busy and time was not lost through waiting for instructions from Nehemiah. It is folly for the officers of a church not to ease their workload by delegating some of their duties to other believers. The elders and deacons may fear that the work will not be performed according to their methods or with their expertise! But how can inexperienced Christians and new converts learn and mature if they are never trusted with some service for the Lord? A young Christian could helpfully be trained by working at the side of an older believer who is both wise and patient. It has been said that 'Today's leaders were yesterday's novices.'[3]

Co-operation

There was co-operation between people from different places and various walks of life. 'The only distinction recognized is that of belonging to the people of God and being engaged in his business.'[4] Nehemiah mentions the priests (3:1) and the rulers (e.g. 3:12,16,17); neither group thought it was beneath their dignity to dirty their hands alongside the working people to erect the wall of Jerusalem. The goldsmiths, renowned for their intricate craftsmanship, turned their hands to the cumbersome chore of bricklaying (3:8,31). Perfume-makers (3:8), temple servants (3:26), merchants (3:32) and **'the guard at the East Gate'** (3:29) all played a rôle in the building project. In the same manner every Christian has some contribution to make in the Lord's work.

The apostle Paul teaches us that the triune God allocates Christians to, and equips each one for, his or her ministry: 'There are different kinds of gifts, but the same Spirit. There are different kinds of service, but the same Lord. There are different kinds of working, but the same God works all of them in all men.' Paul concludes his list of the various gifts with these words: 'All these are the work of one and the same Spirit, and he gives them to each one, just as he determines' (1 Cor. 12:4-6,11). Some of these gifts were confined to the apostolic age and were given to facilitate the rapid spread of the gospel. However, this does not alter the fact that it is God alone who grants gifts to his people and that he selects the sphere of service for each one of them. We ought not to covet someone else's gift, or despise and neglect the gift which we have received from him.

'Shallum ... ruler of a half-district of Jerusalem' enlisted the **'help of his daughters'** (3:12). 'Women were rarely mentioned in the Near East and when their activities are recorded in the Bible, it indicates something very significant.

These young women showed that they were not afraid to do work normally assigned to men.'[5] Christian women should be encouraged to do more than make cups of tea at church anniversaries! Godly ladies played a vital part in the life of the New Testament church, women who were well known for 'helping those in trouble' and who devoted themselves 'to all kinds of good deeds' (1 Tim. 5:10; cf. Titus 2:3-5; Rom. 16:1-2,12). Do the churches to which we belong stimulate the ladies to develop spiritual ministries?

There was collaboration between the citizens of Jerusalem and the men from Jericho (3:2), Tekoa (3:5), Gibeon and Mizpah (3:7), Zanoah (3:13), Beth Hakkerem (3:14), Beth Zur (3:16) and Keilah (3:17). These men did not allow their own interests to keep them away. Will they be an indictment to us because of our lack of zeal for the cause of God?

Conceit

Most of the labourers 'worked with all their heart' (4:6), but the nobles of Tekoa **'would not put their shoulders to the work under their supervisors'** (3:5). The AV translates 'shoulders' as 'necks', which suggests (when compared with Scriptures such as Ps. 75:5) that the refusal of these nobles to work with **'the men of Tekoa'** was because of their 'petty pride rather than half-heartedness'.[6] It seems to me that most divisions within churches can be traced back to pride.

Commendation

Nehemiah took a personal interest in each one of his workers. They were not just statistics, but people whom he knew by name and whose individual efforts were highly valued by him.

The governor picked out some for special commendation —
for example, Malkijah and Hasshub, who **'repaired another
section'** (3:11), and Baruch who **'zealously repaired another section'** (3:20). The expression 'repaired another section' is found six times in the space of twelve verses (3:19,20,
21,24,27,30). Nehemiah does not forget to jot down in his
memoirs that **'Hanun and the residents of Zanoah'** not only
rebuilt **'the Valley Gate'**, but they also **'repaired five hundred yards'** (450 metres) **'of the wall as far as the Dung
Gate'** (3:13). The Dung Gate was fixed single-handedly by
'Malkijah son of Recab' (3:14). The men of Tekoa made up
for the arrogance and laziness of their leaders by pushing
themselves to restore a further section of the wall (3:5,27).

We ought, like Nehemiah, to be careful to give praise to
whom it is due. An occasional word of appreciation may
prevent some hard-pressed Christian from discouragement.
We have a tendency to take for granted the conscientious
Christian who gets on with his or her duties without fuss and
complaint. When such a believer is ill or dies we then discover
the extent of their sacrificial and devoted service on behalf of
the Lord's people. A day is coming when our Master in heaven
will reward every one of his trustworthy servants.

It is instructive to note that Nehemiah does not draw
attention to his own part in the building of the wall. The Judean
governor was happy to give others a place in the spotlight and
himself remain in the shadows. This is in keeping with the
teaching of the wise man Solomon: 'Let another praise you,
and not your own mouth; someone else, and not your own lips'
(Prov. 27:2).

Completion

The result of the Jews' co-ordination and co-operation was
that the wall of Jerusalem was completed in the surprisingly

brief period of fifty-two days (6:15). It is amazing what can be achieved by churches when all the members are committed to the Lord and to each other.

16.
'Our God will fight for us!'

Please read Nehemiah chapter 4

We read in Nehemiah 3 that the Jews began building the walls of Jerusalem; when we turn to chapter 4 we discover that this project was carried out in the face of ruthless and unrelenting opposition. The instigators of this unprovoked attack were two of the evil trio whom we met in Nehemiah 2: Sanballat (4:1) and Tobiah (4:3). They were assisted in their vicious assault on God's people by **'the Arabs, the Ammonites and the men of Ashdod'** (4:7), who lived in the land once occupied by the Philistines, long-standing enemies of the Jews.

The builders were encircled, with Sanballat in the north, Tobiah in the east, the Arabs in the south and the Ashdodites posing a threat in the west. However, God did not desert the Jews but gave them strength and courage to come through their various trials. He supported his people not only because of his special love for them, but also because he had his eye on the future of the Jewish race. The survival of the Jews was tied in with the salvation of the elect drawn from all nations.

The leadership of Nehemiah and the faith of the Jews were tested to the limits. Nehemiah's handling of harassment, and the subsequent temptation to discouragement, is full of instruction for those feeling the pressure of the Lord's work. The way that we deal with frustrations in Christian work and in our personal lives shows what kind of people we are.

The ridicule of Sanballat and Tobiah (4:1-3)

Anger was the root cause of Sanballat's ridicule (4:1). But why should the restoration of the derelict walls of Jerusalem produce such a violent outburst from the governor of Samaria? Cyril Barber explains why Sanballat saw Jerusalem as a threat to Samaria: 'One of the main highways linking the Tigris-Euphrates river valley to the north with Egypt in the south and Philistia in the west, passes through Jerusalem. With Jerusalem once more a well-protected city, its very location will attract trade; and gone will be Samaria's economic supremacy.'[1]

So Sanballat, with Tobiah, in the company of a crowd of supporters, marched with his army into the city of Jerusalem to launch an attack on the Jews. The patronage of King Artaxerxes restricted Sanballat to a verbal onslaught. However, it soon became apparent that the Samaritan governor was adept in the use of the weapon of the tongue!

Sanballat opens his diatribe with wounding sarcasm: **'What are those feeble Jews doing? Will they restore their wall?'** (4:2). He attempts to put the Jews down and destroy their self-esteem. Kidner suggests that the point of **'Will they offer sacrifices?'** is 'Are these fanatics going to *pray* the wall up? It's their only hope!'[2] Sarcasm is rapidly followed up with a jibe: **'Will they finish in a day?'** The implication of this question is that the task is too large and will therefore never be completed. The impossibility of the job in hand is pressed home: **'Can they bring the stones back to life from those heaps of rubble — burned as they are?'** The burnt and crumbling limestone walls remained in a state of disrepair for almost a century.

Tobiah joins in the fun: **'What they are building — if even a fox climbed up on it, he would break down their wall of stones!'** (4:3). Tobiah dismisses the Jews as a bunch of amateur builders whose wall would soon fall down. Taking our cue from Jesus, who called King Herod a fox (Luke 13:31-32), we may say that Sanballat and Tobiah were as cunning as foxes, but all their machinations could not knock down Nehemiah's wall!

The response of Nehemiah (4:4-6)

How did Nehemiah counteract this malicious slander and disheartening derision? It was a critical moment. The future of the building undertaking was in the balance. Nehemiah prayed! This ought not to surprise us — he prayed when he received distressing news from his brother about the Jews in Jerusalem (ch. 1), and also when King Artaxerxes demanded to know the reason for his sad face (ch. 2). Prayer was the instinctive reaction of Nehemiah when confronted with a crisis, unlike many people who only pray in desperation when everything else has failed. Nehemiah poured out his heart to God rather than entering into futile arguments with his opponents. He believed that the rebuilding of the wall was God's work and he would bring it to a successful end. Later Nehemiah reassured the builders with the words: 'Our God will fight for us!' (4:20).

There are two aspects to this prayer of Nehemiah.

1. He appeals to the merciful God (4:4)

The words, **'Hear us,'** may indicate that Nehemiah's prayer was a public one as he pleaded with God on behalf of the nation. The basis of his plea was God's unique relationship with his people — **'our God'**. Surely God would come to the relief of his own people who were **'despised'**? The merciful God declares in his Word that he feels all the pains of his suffering people. One passage which makes this point is Isaiah

63:9, which refers back to God's gracious dealings with the Israelites in the wilderness:

> In all their distress he too was distressed,
>   and the angel of his presence saved them.
> In his love and mercy he redeemed them;
>   he lifted them up and carried them
>   all the days of old.

'The angel of his presence' is none other than the 'man of sorrows' who is 'familiar with suffering', the Lord Jesus Christ (Isa. 53:3).[3]

2. He beseeches the God of justice (4:4-5)

Nehemiah prays that his antagonists may themselves receive the evil which they wished for the people of God. He asks God to mete out his wrath on Sanballat and his allies. Similar sentiments are expressed by the Judean governor in later chapters (5:13; 6:14; 13:25; cf. 10:29). His language is reminiscent of the imprecatory prayers of David in which he calls on God to punish the wicked. An example of this kind of prayer is found in Psalm 109, which is said to be the most imprecatory of all the psalms. How are we to explain these petitions of David and Nehemiah? Are they harsh and vindictive? The prayers of these Old Testament men seem to be in jarring contrast to the words of Jesus, who taught us to forgive those who offend us (Matt. 6:12,14-15). As we grapple with the difficulties arising from these prayers we ought not to overlook the fact that David, the author of most of the imprecatory psalms, refused to hurt King Saul, one of his worst enemies, when he had the opportunity to do so (1 Sam. 24; 26). He was willing to forgive Saul and made every effort to be at peace with him.

Several attempts have been made to tone down the apparent harshness of these imprecatory supplications. Some writers take the view that these passages are prophecies rather than actual prayers. Others propound the idea that God allowed these prayers though he does not really approve of them. Others have proposed that these prayers were suitable for the godly in the Old Testament era but are no longer appropriate for believers living after the life and death of Jesus Christ, the loving Saviour. This argument is flawed because there are various occasions recorded in the New Testament when the apostles called down God's wrath on the wicked (Acts 1:20; 5:1-11; 13:10-11; Rom. 11:9-10; 2 Tim. 4:14-15). It has even been suggested that these prayers were the result of the excitable temperament of men who lived in the Middle East. It was sinful culture rather than grace speaking! But all these interpretations are inadequate.[4]

These 'problem prayers' can only be understood when we realize that Nehemiah and David were concerned with the glory of God. When Sanballat and Tobiah mocked the Jews, God's chosen people, they were in actual fact scorning God himself. These two evil men had **'thrown insults in the face of the builders'** (4:5). The NIV note reads, 'They have provoked *you* to anger' (italics mine). This alternative reading, adopted by the translators of the Authorized Version, gets to the crux of the matter. The Amplified Bible blends the two readings together: 'They have vexed [with alarm] the builders and provoked You.' God's anger against Sanballat and Tobiah was not irreversible; their repentance would guarantee his mercy!

We may derive encouragement from Nehemiah's prayer. God takes a personal interest in all that happens to us. We are precious to him and he is offended when some unbeliever pokes fun at our profession of him. We also learn from Nehemiah's prayer that 'The secret of overcoming opposition lies in our relationship with the Lord.'[5]

The immediate response of Nehemiah to the mockery of Sanballat was to pray. Then he urged the builders to get back to their work. **'So we rebuilt the wall'** (4:6). 'The sturdy simplicity of that statement, and of the behaviour it records, makes Sanballat and his friends suddenly appear rather small and shrill, dwarfed by the faith, unity and energy of the weak.'[6] Nehemiah would not allow the Hebrews to sit around licking their wounds. He urged them to pick up their trowels and start building again. So today busy Christians will not have time to fret about the taunts of the ungodly.

The essential element demanded in any kind of project, secular or spiritual, is enshrined in the words at the end of verse 6: **'The people worked with all their heart.'** What would happen if we had Christians of this calibre in every church in our land? Too often our service for the Lord is half-hearted and therefore so pathetic.

The reaction of the Jews (4:7-15)

When Sanballat and his allies realized that their ridicule had failed to stop the work they threatened the Jews with violence (4:8). This intimidation was dealt with by earnest prayer for divine assistance and increased labour on the wall (4:9). There was prayer and perspiration! Prayer without work is presumption, and work without prayer is self-confidence. We must pray because we accomplish nothing without God's power, but at the same time we are to labour for God as if everything depended on our efforts.

As the Jews pressed on with their assignment they could hear the relentless and disheartening words of three groups pounding their eardrums. Some of their own number, who had prayed with them for God's help, were still overwhelmed at the enormity of the task: **'The strength of the labourers is giving out, and there is so much rubble that we cannot**

rebuild the wall' (4:10). When does realism become pessi-
mism? It is true that we should weigh up carefully the difficulties in any spiritual enterprise, but we ought not to let our
evaluation depress and defeat us. Nothing is too hard for our
God! (Jer. 32:17).

The builders were also bombarded with further menacing
words from their adversaries: **'Before they know it or see us,
we will be right there among them and will kill them and
put an end to the work'** (4:11). The third group was comprised of Jews who had swallowed the propaganda of the
opposition: **'Wherever you turn, they will attack us'** (4:12).
They repeated their dismal message **'ten times'**; sometimes
our friends are our worst enemies! Exhaustion ('The strength
of the labourers is giving out'), fear ('They will attack us') and
incessant harassment were getting through to some of God's
people. When we are drained of energy and prone to fear and
depression we must not give up serving the Lord lest we lose
the fruit of our strenuous labour over many years.

Once again Nehemiah demonstrated his mettle in his handling of this predicament. Nehemiah dealt with the situation in
three ways: firstly, he improved the defence of the walls
(4:13); then he thought seriously, and no doubt prayed also,
about the current problems; after which he spoke words of
reassurance to **'the nobles, the officials and the rest of the
people'** (4:14). The beginning of verse 14 may imply that
Nehemiah actually saw their adversaries advancing in the
distance: **'After I looked things over...'** Whatever he saw, the
courageous Nehemiah was not panic-stricken because by faith
he saw the presence of God.

Nehemiah perceived the mood of the builders as he galvan-
ized them into action: **'Don't be afraid of them.'** They were
to fix their thoughts on the Lord **'who is great and awesome'** (4:14; cf. 1:5). The fear of the Lord is the cure for the fear
of man. Renewed strength was derived from God to fight on

behalf of their families and homes (4:14); therefore Nehemiah records, **'We all returned to the wall, each to his own work'** (4:15). Nehemiah, as ever, was careful to give the credit to God for overturning the spiteful schemes of Sanballat: **'We were aware of their plot and that God had frustrated it'** (4:15).

'Our God will fight for us!' (4:16-23)

The entire city of Jerusalem was converted into an armed camp. Nehemiah arranged the men into two groups: those who **'did the work'** and others who **'were equipped with spears, shields, bows and armour'** (4:16). The working shift were also armed: they **'did their work with one hand and held a weapon in the other, and each of the builders wore his sword at his side as he worked'** (4:17-18). Those who lived in the surrounding cities were obliged to stay overnight in the capital in case of an invasion (4:21-22). Each person, worker or guard, kept an ear open for the warning sound of the trumpet summoning them to fight an invading foe (4:18-20). The business of the Jews was so urgent and the danger of a raid so pressing that they did not even have time to change their clothes or to sleep (4:22-23).[7]

The despondency of verse 10 was replaced with renewed vigour for their God-given mandate to erect the walls of Jerusalem. What had brought about this change? It was a fresh realization of the presence of their mighty defender: **'Our God will fight for us!'** (4:20). God fought for his people, not because he was the tribal god of the Jews, but rather to move forward his predestined plan to bring salvation to sinful men and women through Christ, born within the pale of the Jewish race.

We too are engaged in a warfare, 'not against flesh and blood, but against the rulers, against the authorities, against the powers of this dark world and against the spiritual forces of evil in the heavenly realms' (Eph. 6:12). The apostle Paul's teaching in this verse is that behind all human antagonism to the gospel message and against ourselves as Christians is the might of Satan and his powerful regiment of demons. But the Lord who has enlisted us in his army is more powerful than the devil. Our divine Captain equips us with armour and gives us strength to conquer (Eph. 6:10-11). In the language of Nehemiah, 'Our God will fight for us!' God's work, then and now, is accomplished by faith — **'Our God will fight for us'** (4:20) — and hard work —**'So we continued the work'** (4:21).

The confidence of the Christian is given expression in the hymn of Edith Cherry:

> We rest on thee, our Shield and our Defender!
> We go not forth alone against the foe;
> Strong in thy strength, safe in thy keeping tender,
> We rest on thee, and in thy name we go.
>
> We go in faith, our own great weakness feeling,
> And needing more each day thy grace to know;
> Yet from our hearts a song of triumph pealing:
> 'We rest on thee, and in thy name we go.'[8]

One day the Lord will give to his faithful soldiers a crown of righteousness! (2 Tim. 4:8).

17.
Rich man, poor man

Please read Nehemiah chapter 5

The rôle of leadership is never easy! This was the experience of Nehemiah, whose attention was diverted from the enemies of God's people and the building of the walls of Jerusalem to the pressing problems of hunger and exploitation. Now the erection of the walls came to a screeching halt. This time the troublemakers were not foreign adversaries but some 'get-rich-quick' Jews taking advantage of a famine to make some easy money from their own kinsmen. This new threat struck 'at the exiles' most precious asset, their unity'.[1] How would Nehemiah come to grips with this setback?

Churches go through similar periods. We resist the attacks of the devil coming at us from unbelievers, only to discover that Satan is now using fellow Christians to breed discontent and discouragement within our own ranks. Internal conflicts sap us of strength and impede our endeavours to reach the unconverted.

Nehemiah receives complaints (5:1-5)

Three groups of labourers and landowners came to Nehemiah with their grievances **'against their Jewish brothers'** (5:1). These complaints were substantiated by their wives, who were struggling to feed their ravenous children (5:2). The 'shrill voices' of these women 'add to the intensity of the meeting' with Nehemiah.[2]

1. The labourers

Manpower had been rechannelled from raising crops to building walls, resulting in a shortage of food. This situation was aggravated by three things: firstly, the large families of the labourers (5:2); secondly, the widespread famine (5:3); and thirdly, the considerable tax payable to the Persian king (5:4). Some of the labourers may have felt that 'Too much was being sacrificed to Nehemiah's project. "After all," as such citizens might have put it, "you can't eat walls".'[3]

2. The landowners

The landowning farmers were compelled to sell everything they could lay their hands on to raise money for food (5:3). Some had no choice but to pay mortgages with exorbitant rates of interest to the 'loan sharks' (5:4,11). Failure to pay back the mortgages resulted in the unscrupulous money-lenders selling the sons and daughters of the debtors into slavery (5:5). This kind of treatment was all the more galling and despicable because it came from the hands of their 'Jewish brothers' (5:1), those who were **'of the same flesh and blood ... our country-men'** (5:5). These men also had children —**'Our sons are as good as theirs'** — and should therefore have felt the anguish of the parents whose sons and daughters were dragged away and sold as slaves. **'We are powerless, because our fields and our vineyards belong to others'** (5:5), was the depressing lament of the demoralized Jews as they surveyed their land.

Nehemiah responds to the complaints (5:6-7)

1. His sympathy

Though Nehemiah was extremely busy with the wall-building enterprise his reaction was not one of impatience or irritability, but of sympathy and interest. He dropped everything to concentrate his thoughts on the outrage of his workers. Their grievances touched him deeply. Christian leaders who brush aside valid complaints and constructive criticism are likely to reap more serious trouble later. This is rather like ignoring a leak in the bathroom. A few moments today repairing the leak will save a hefty bill tomorrow when the whole bathroom is flooded with water! It is better to nip in the bud any potential difficulties within a church rather than let them bloom into a major crisis in the future. However, we should act only after careful consideration. Nehemiah tells us that **'When I heard their outcry and these charges ... I pondered them in my mind'** (5:6,7); then, and only then, did he set about solving the problem.

2. His anger

Nehemiah was **'very angry'** (5:6) when he heard of the rich Jews oppressing their poor countrymen. 'His anger was the measure of his concern, or love,' but this concern was 'controlled and constructive'.⁴ It is not sinful for a Christian to express his anger. Jesus himself gave vent to this emotion (Mark 3:5; John 2:13-17), but we must be on our guard lest our wrath boil over into sinful anger (Eph. 4:26-27). We need to remember the words of the wise man Solomon: 'Better a patient man than a warrior, a man who controls his temper than one who takes a city' (Prov. 16:32)

It was the injustice of the rich Jews oppressing the poorer members of their own race that triggered off Nehemiah's anger. Ought not the injustices of our age cause us to be angry? For example, when we see on television people starving in the developing world and we know that tons of food are wasted in the Western world, we ought to be angry; when we hear of children who are physically, sexually, or emotionally abused we should be angry; when we read that hundreds of unborn babies are aborted every year then we have a reason for righteous anger. Our anger is unproductive if it does not lead to some attempt to deal with what gave rise to it. The sequel to Nehemiah's displeasure was a solution to the problem.

Nehemiah's anger, directed against the rich oppressors of the poor, had its roots in the teaching of God's Word, though this is not specifically stated in the text. Nehemiah the Jew would have been familiar with passages such as Deuteronomy 23:19-20, which forbade a Jew to charge a fellow Jew interest, and Leviticus 25:10,14-17,25-28, in which God commanded his people to release Jewish slaves and to return property to its original owners in the Year of Jubilee. Other passages which may have been recalled by Nehemiah at this time were those in which God, who has a tender love for the poor, demands that his people display compassion towards the needy (such as Deut. 15:1-11).

We ought to be irate about social injustice, and even more angry that Satan enslaves sinners and blinds their minds so that they reject the teaching of the Bible and rush on towards hell (2 Cor. 4:3-4; 2 Tim. 2:26). If Christians, who still have a sinful nature, are vexed because of the social evils which they see all around them, and at the rejection of God's Word on every hand, how much more must God, who is holy, be displeased because of sin?

Nehemiah resolves the complaints (5:7-13)

1. He confronts the nobles (5:7-8)

Nehemiah did not flinch from the unpleasant task of confronting the nobles with their misdemeanour. Their transgression against God was notorious; therefore he convened **'a large meeting to deal with them'** (5:7). This assembly was not to be some kind of 'public enquiry' behind closed doors with the outcome kept secret and no positive steps taken to address the underlying cause of the conflict. The culprits were faced head on and their sins publicly exposed. Nehemiah emphasized the enormity of the nobles' wickedness in two ways: firstly he accused them of exploiting their **'own countrymen ... our Jewish brothers'**; then he charged them with frustrating all his efforts to release their fellow Jews from slavery. Some of the people sold back to Nehemiah by the non-Jewish nations had first been traded to them by the callous rich Jews. This made their sin all the more disgraceful.

Church officers will sometimes have to investigate delicate matters relating to the discipline of errant believers. They must resist the temptation to cover up deviant conduct; rather they should ask God for courage to deal thoroughly with the issue and pray that the sinful believer will repent of his transgressions. However, before spiritual leaders initiate any disciplinary proceedings the guilt of the offender must be firmly established. The nobles could not refute the charges which Nehemiah laid against them because their sins were infamous and their own consciences condemned them so that **'They kept quiet, because they could find nothing to say'** (5:8).

2. He calls the nobles to 'walk in the fear of our God' (5:9-10)

Nehemiah describes this fear as 'reverence for God' in verse 15. The 'fear of God' may be defined as an awareness of the

majestic holiness of God and a realization of our own sinfulness. The consequence of this fear is obedience to all the
commands of God contained in his Word. Nehemiah was
compassionate and generous to God's people because he had
this awe of God, whereas the rich had no respect for their
fellow Jews because they had no respect for God. Therefore
they were squeezing their Jewish brothers for all they could get
rather than offering interest-free loans as Nehemiah was
doing. The person who possesses the 'fear of God' remembers
that his treatment of other people will be assessed by God on
the Day of Judgement. Jesus taught in the parable of the sheep
and goats that kindness shown to his people is kindness shown
to himself. We cannot be saved by our good deeds, but we are
certainly not Christians without them (Matt. 25:31-46; 1 John
4:20-21).

The lesson we may draw from the end of verse 9 is that the
professing Christian who lacks this fear of God invites the
taunts of unbelievers against his religion and his God. The
most unholy sinner is quick to label the inconsistent Christian
a sanctimonious hypocrite and thereby excuse his own evil
behaviour.

3. He commands the nobles to promise compensation (5:10-13)

Nehemiah does not want to leave the nobles in any doubt about
what they must do: **'But let the exacting of usury stop! Give
back to them immediately their fields, vineyards, olive
groves and houses, and also the usury you are charging
them...'** (5:10-11). The reference to **'the hundredth part of
the money'** (5:11) is 'a refund either of interest charged on the
loans or the income derived by the creditors from the property
they have taken in pledge'.[5]

The overwhelming response of the officials, **'We will give it back ... We will do as you say'**, was acted on at once by Nehemiah as he summoned the priests to witness the promises of **'the nobles and officials'** (5:12). Nehemiah was not going to allow them to have second thoughts and then change their minds! The solemnity of the oath was impressed on the nobles by Nehemiah's gesture of shaking his robe, indicating that God would 'shake out from his home and possessions each one who did not keep the oath'[6] (5:13; cf. Matt. 10:14; Acts 18:5-6). The rich who did not assist the poor would themselves become poor.

Why did these men who had so much to lose agree so readily with Nehemiah's demands? There may have been various contributing factors which brought about this alteration, such as a feeling of guilt, or the courage of Nehemiah, but the origin of this turnabout was surely God's power at work in their hearts. The Lord who moved the heart of Cyrus to allow the first batch of exiles to return to their homeland (Ezra 1:1), and who prompted Artaxerxes to rescind his decree outlawing the rebuilding of Jerusalem, so that Nehemiah was free to go into Judah as governor and wall-builder (2:1-9), now stirred these officials to heed Nehemiah's appeal. This God was slotting together all the events in the Middle East to bring about the birth of Christ, in order to save his people from their sins (Matt. 1:21). He still controls the affairs of men and the timetable of history. Everything is moving forward to the return of the Lord Jesus Christ to whom every knee will bow (Phil. 2:9-11).

The **'whole assembly'** vocally added their assent to the vows of the nobles and officials, and later performed the promises made (5:13). Nehemiah notes in his diary that this memorable day concluded with a crescendo of praise to God. The day which began with pain ends with praise!

Nehemiah's leadership (5:14-19)

At this stage in his narrative Nehemiah reflects on his style of leadership during his twelve years as governor from 445 to 433 B.C. What principles shaped the character of this governor of Judah and man of God throughout those twelve years?

1. He was selfless and generous

Nehemiah was entitled to levy a food allowance from the Judeans but chose to cover his entertainment expenses out of his own pocket rather than place **'a heavy burden on the people'** (5:14-15). Verse 18 reveals that his food bill was an enormous one! The governor of Judah was renowned among **'the surrounding nations'** for his lavish hospitality and magnificent generosity (5:17). It is evident from these verses that Nehemiah had private resources accumulated during his service as the cupbearer to King Artaxerxes I. God blessed Nehemiah with prosperity but he did not make a god of his affluence, but rather used it for the glory of God as he served others. The cordiality of Nehemiah is set in striking contrast to the selfish and greedy outlook of some of the previous governors (5:15).

Whether we have much or little of material prosperity we ought to copy the example of Nehemiah and be selfless and generous. We who have freely received the grace of God should freely share with others whatever we possess (Matt. 10:8). We may open our homes to a brother or sister in Christ and discover that we have entertained an angel! (Heb. 13:2). Abraham literally welcomed angels without realizing it (Gen. 18). Whenever I read Hebrews 13 my mind goes back to December 1978. I was in my third year as a pastor in the East End of London and just five months into married life! At that time I attended a minister's fraternal where I spoke to a pastor whose wife was permanently in hospital with cancer. He seemed so downhearted that my heart went out to him. We invited him to our home. Those few days were ones of precious fellowship which we shall never forget. We felt that we had entertained an angel!

2. *He was single-minded*

Nehemiah jots down in his memoir, **'I devoted myself to the work on this wall. All my men were assembled there for the work'** (5:16). Nothing is accomplished in the Lord's work without this single-mindedness.

3. *He was godly*

The godliness of Nehemiah is encapsulated in the words found in verse 15: **'Their assistants also lorded it over the people. But out of reverence for God I did not act like that.'** His awe of God was the source of his piety and the driving force behind his service for God. Nehemiah was a man who loved God and therefore loved his neighbour as himself (Deut. 6:5; Lev. 19:18; Matt. 22:34-40). It seems to me that 'reverence for God' is missing from so many of our evangelical churches at the present time. I was challenged about my own awareness of God's presence when I read Don Carson's book on the prayers of the apostle Paul. After an examination of various proposals to deal with the spiritual decline within present-day evangelicalism he comments, 'The one thing we most urgently need in Western Christendom is a deeper knowledge of God. We need to know God better.'[7]

Nehemiah's prayer, **'Remember me with favour, O my God'** (5:19), makes it clear that he was a man who was 'motivated by his knowledge of who God is, and strengthened by the assurance of what God can do'.[8] Nehemiah's request should be ours as we build the city of God's church.

18.
Pressure and priorities

Please read Nehemiah chapter 6

In this chapter we meet again with Sanballat, Tobiah and
Geshem, whom we have already encountered in Nehemiah
chapters 2 and 4. Sanballat, the governor of Samaria, Tobiah,
the Ammonite official, and Geshem, the Arab, had underesti-
mated the stamina and resourcefulness of their rival
Nehemiah. The supporters of these wicked men were superior
in strength to Nehemiah's workforce-cum-army, but his reli-
ance was in God, the defender of his people (2:20; 4:20). Now
these enemies whose pride was wounded try different tactics
with the aim of destroying the credibility of Nehemiah in the
eyes of the Jews. Spiritual leaders must expect to be the targets
of attack from Satan and his human allies.

The combined forces lined up to oppose Nehemiah re-
doubled their efforts when they heard that the walls of Jerusalem were rebuilt. All that remained to complete the venture
was to hang the doors in the spaces reserved for them in the
walls. 'The open gateways (1) were the enemy's last hope of
regaining the upper hand without actually mounting a siege,
which would be out of the question against fellow subjects of
Persia.'[1]

Three schemes were concocted in an attempt to defeat
Nehemiah and his workers.

1. Call a truce! (6:1-4)

A letter was sent from Sanballat and Geshem to Nehemiah inviting him to join them in **'one of the villages on the plain of Ono'** (6:2). This letter was a proposition to Nehemiah of peaceful coexistence with his enemies now turned friends. No doubt this offer sounded like good news to the Jews who were weary and hungry. A truce was surely better than constant harassment. But Nehemiah was not fooled. He saw through the plausible invitation; he perceived that **'they were scheming to harm'** him (6:2). The location of this proposed meeting would have aroused Nehemiah's suspicions. The valley of Ono was near the borders of Samaria and not far from Philistia, the country of the Ashdodites, who were associates of Sanballat. The modern Israeli name of Ono is Kafr' Ana and it is situated just east of Tel-Aviv. Nehemiah would not befriend his adversaries. He knew that the leopard does not change its spots.

Nehemiah's reply to the request by Sanballat and Geshem for 'peace talks' in the valley of Ono was: **'I am carrying on a great project and cannot go down. Why should the work stop while I leave it and go down to you?'** (6:3-4). The valley of Ono was more than a day's journey from Jerusalem; therefore if Nehemiah travelled to this location he would waste valuable time needed to push the building work on to its completion. This assignment was too important and too demanding for him to leave; besides his presence was needed in Jerusalem to prevent the nobles and officials going back on their promises (5:11-13). Nehemiah's refusal to desert his work provides us with another example of his single-mindedness (5:16). There was no stratagem employed by his opponents which was allowed to sidetrack him from his God-given task of erecting the city walls. Behind the face of human enemies is our greatest adversary the devil, who has a box full of tricks to distract us from serving God. We are to reckon with his might and be aware of his devices (2 Cor. 2:11; Eph. 6:10-18).

Satan not only instigates opposition, he also presents us with persuasive reasons for spending less time in private devotions and for opting out of Christian service. For example, do we allow secular employment and legitimate recreations to encroach on our time so that God's work is neglected? I remember a Christian man telling me that he has consistently refused promotion so that he can devote himself to the ministry of the church to which he belongs. He is a married man with children who holds a responsible position in a leading financial group in the city of London. His goal in life is not advancing his career or increasing his wealth but his ministry for the Master who died to save him. Nehemiah's reply to Sanballat compels us to consider our priorities.

2. Read a letter! (6:5-9)

Once Sanballat realized that he had failed to entice Nehemiah away from Jerusalem he tried a new and more devious ploy. He sent his aide with a letter to Nehemiah in which he informed him of gossip that the Judean governor was plotting treason against Artaxerxes. These stories were attested by **'Geshem'**, who **'says it is true'** (6:6). Sanballat came in the guise of a friend offering Nehemiah an opportunity to clear his name: **'Now this report will get back to the king; so come, let us confer together'** (6:7), but in reality the open letter was designed to ferment the rumours rather than allay them. The charges were downright lies, but Sanballat was working on the principle that 'There is no smoke without fire.' It is a sad fact of life that 'People are always quick to believe the worst about others.'² Would Nehemiah be blackmailed, through fear of losing his reputation, into a compromise with Sanballat and his cronies?

Nehemiah's priority when invited to leave Jerusalem was to carry on working for God; his priority when his character was maligned was to pray to that same God. His petition, preceded by an open denial of the accusation, **'Nothing like what you are saying is happening; you are just making it up out of your head'** (6:8), was simple and to the point: **'Now strengthen my hands'** (6:9). He brings God into the picture. This was something which Sanballat had not bargained for! The feeble drooping hands of Nehemiah and his builders were made strong by the mighty God of heaven. There is not only a contrast in verse 9 between the weakness of the Jews and the strength of God; there is also an implied contrast between the puniness of Sanballat and the power of God. It is utterly futile for anyone to set himself up against God. The attempt to defeat God's people is doomed to failure. When we are tempted to be afraid then we need to recall the words of the apostle Paul: 'We are more than conquerors through him who loved us' (Rom. 8:37), and the context of those encouraging words (Rom. 8:28-39).

Nehemiah's conscience was free of guilt; therefore he did not hesitate to plead with God for divine assistance to remain firm in this painful trial. A clear conscience gives us boldness when we supplicate the holy God. Nehemiah was convinced that the righteous God who sees into the heart would vindicate him.

Many years after Nehemiah's time the apostle Peter wrote to believers scattered throughout northern Turkey who were struggling with misunderstanding. He directed their thoughts to the Lord Jesus Christ, who was falsely arraigned: 'When they hurled their insults at him, he did not retaliate; when he suffered, he made no threats. Instead, he entrusted himself to

him who judges justly' (1 Peter 2:23; cf. Luke 23:2,5). The
sinless and suffering Saviour left his honour in the hands of his
heavenly Father. We must learn to copy his example if we
experience the distress of slander. The attitude of Nehemiah
and of Christ will guard us against the snare of resentment and
revenge.

3. Meet a priest! (6:10-14)

One day Nehemiah received a request to visit a man named
'Shemaiah son of Delaiah'. He may have been connected
with the family of Delaiah mentioned in the list of exiles who
returned from Babylon in the days of Zerubbabel (Ezra 2:60).
Assuming that he was the same Shemaiah of whom we read in
Nehemiah 10:8, he was a priest. Shemaiah was unable to call
on Nehemiah because he was **'shut in at his home'** for some
unspecified cause (6:10). 'The fact that Shemaiah would
propose going to the Temple shows that his disability, if it
existed at all, was only temporary, hardly a sufficient reason
to bring the governor to his house.'[3]

Shemaiah tried to engender fear in the heart of Nehemiah
as he suggested that the governor ought to seek sanctuary
within the temple: **'Let us meet in the house of God, inside
the temple, and let us close the temple doors, because men
are coming to kill you — by night they are coming to kill
you'** (6:10). The cunning priest presents his proposal as a
prophecy, a message from God, to persuade Nehemiah. How
could he disobey the voice of God? But Nehemiah discerned
that Shemaiah was a false prophet who was the hired spokesperson of Sanballat (6:12-13). Modern false prophets often
come in the guise of money-motivated charismatic
televangelists. It is sad that many sincere believers are so
gullible that they accept without question the extravagant and

unsubstantiated claims of healings made by some of these televangelists. Such Christians lack the discernment of Nehemiah derived from his knowledge of God's Word and his fellowship with God through prayer.

The idea of running away from danger was abhorrent to the courageous Nehemiah. His question, **'Should one like me go into the temple to save his life?'** (6:11) expressed Nehemiah's humility and his obedience to God's Word. He was not a priest and therefore had no rights to go into the areas of the temple restricted to the priests. Any violation of the divine regulation concerning entry into the Holy Place was punishable with death (Num. 1:51; 3:10). The command of God was more important than the word of a man, even though that man was a priest who claimed a supernatural gift of prophecy. Nehemiah, like the apostles after him, feared God rather than men (5:9,15; Acts 5:29).

Nehemiah's words in verse 12, **'I realized that God had not sent him'**, may indicate that he did not immediately grasp Shemaiah's wicked intentions. Slowly the truth dawned on him that this was another of Sanballat's manoeuvres to **'give me a bad name to discredit me'** (6:13). His aim was to brand Nehemiah as a coward and a law-breaker. This encounter with Shemaiah left Nehemiah acutely aware of his own need and the subtlety of his opponents; therefore he appealed again to God for his protection in the punishment of his foes (6:14).

Shemaiah was not the only person in alliance with Sanballat and Tobiah. Nehemiah mentions in his prayer **'the prophetess Noadiah and the rest of the prophets who have been trying to intimidate me'** (6:14). Noadiah was of the same ilk as the prophetesses who lived at the time of the seventy-year exile (Ezek. 13:17-23). In sharp contrast to these fraudulent prophetesses we read in the Old Testament of Miriam (Exod. 15:19-21) and Deborah (Judg. 4; 5) who used their gifts not for sordid gain or prestige but for the glory of

God. We have read in a previous chapter of the daughters of
Shallum who helped him build a section of the Jerusalem wall
(3:12). Women can be a powerful influence for good (such as
Selina the Countess of Huntingdon, supporter and friend of the
eighteenth-century evangelist, George Whitefield) or for evil
(such as Mary Baker Eddy, founder of the Christian Science
movement in 1866). There is some truth in the old adage, 'The
hand that rocks the cradle is the hand that rules the world.'[4] It
has been calculated that Ezra and Nehemiah between them use
367 personal names, but only one is the name of a woman —
Noadiah the prophetess. Curiously enough, the same name is
used of a man in Ezra 8:33.[5]

Achievement and intimidation (6:15-19)

The conspiracies of Sanballat not only failed to halt the
building, they also made Nehemiah all the more determined to
finish the walls of the capital city. It must have been with a sigh
of relief and gratitude to God that he wrote in his diary, **'So the
wall was completed on the twenty-fifth of Elul, in fifty-two
days'** (6:15). Elul (August/September) was the sixth month of
the Jewish sacred year, which began with Nisan (March/April)
(2:1). All the events of chapters 2-6 were crowded into a space
of six months. The actual building of the walls was accomplished in less than two of those months!

How did Nehemiah attain so much in so little time? He was
convinced that God had instructed him to build the walls of
Jerusalem. Therefore he would not permit conflict among
God's people (ch. 5) or opposition from the ungodly (ch. 6) to
discourage him so that he gave up his labour for the Lord. We
should also take into account the fact that there was a vast
workforce drawn from all the areas around Jerusalem and that
the ruins of the previous wall contained large quantities of

stones which may have been stockpiled ready for use. God has called us to build the city of his church; we too must not let ourselves be deflected from this great task. Lethargy and procrastination are twin enemies which the church has constantly to combat.

The speed of the task made Nehemiah's antagonists lose their confidence and forced them to acknowledge that **'This work had been done with the help of our God'** (6:16). 'Viewing Nehemiah's victory as their defeat, the self-confidence of the opposition was considerably diminished.'[6] Nevertheless, Tobiah the Ammonite still continued to cause trouble (6:17-18). It must have been tiresome for the Judean governor to hear the relatives of Tobiah boasting of his good deeds, and **'telling him what I said'** (6:19). The names of Tobiah ('Jah is good') and his son Jehohanan ('Jehovah has shown mercy') suggest that the Ammonite official was a nominal believer in God. The presence of nominal Christians within a church is far more dangerous than enemies outside because they bring their unspiritual reasoning and worldly viewpoint with them.

Nehemiah's commitment to the work of God had long-term repercussions. Remember that the defence of Jerusalem and the survival of the Jewish race were stepping-stones to the coming of the Messiah-Saviour. The church today is reaping the benefit of Nehemiah's faithfulness to the Lord. Will future generations praise God for our loyalty to him or will they suffer the consequences of our compromise?

19.
The new community

It was an astounding feat to complete the Jerusalem wall-building programme in just under two months. One problem remained: who was going to live in the rebuilt city and defend it from attack? The laudable commitment which the Jews manifested while erecting the wall was now called for in the repopulation of Jerusalem. The Jews who moved to Jerusalem were expected to subordinate their own interests to the will of God for the benefit of his people. Who would be willing to make this sacrifice and pull up their roots to resettle in the capital city? Christians too ought to be more solicitous about the progress of the church and the glory of God than about their own particular spheres of service. The ministry of individual believers and churches is of the utmost importance to the Lord. Nevertheless our labours are only part of the overall global work of God which spans the centuries from the creation until its consummation at the second advent of our Lord Jesus Christ.

The **'large and spacious'** Jerusalem hardly merited the name of city because so few people lived there (7:4). How the governor of Judah came to grips with this quandary is the subject of Nehemiah chapters 7, 11 and 12. But first it was imperative for him to organize the government of the new community.

New leaders (7:1-3)

The success or failure of any enterprise, secular or spiritual, will to some extent depend on the strength or weakness of the leadership selected. Therefore the sagacious Nehemiah put his mind to the issue of the administration of the capital city. Firstly, **'The gatekeepers and the singers and the Levites were appointed'** (7:1). The spiritual oversight was sorted out before the secular because the main reason for the restoration of Jerusalem was that God might be worshipped in his temple. Do the adoration and service of God take precedence in our lives?

David, in former days, entrusted to the gatekeepers the task of 'guarding the gates of the house of the Lord' and 'the responsibility for the rooms and treasuries in the house of God'; they also opened the temple doors each morning and performed various other functions allocated to them (1 Chron. 9:17-34). Now Nehemiah gave to the gatekeepers wider duties, outside of the temple: **'The gates of Jerusalem are not to be opened until the sun is hot'** (7:3). There is some debate among the scholars about the precise meaning of this verse. It may mean, 'Don't leave the gates open in the midday siesta,' or 'The gates should be opened late and closed early.'[1] Later the Levites were commanded to 'guard the gates in order to keep the Sabbath day holy' (13:22), a necessary injunction because of Sabbath-day traders camping near the city (13:15-22).

It was in the interest of each resident to comply with Nehemiah's instructions to once again guard the section of the wall nearest to his own home (7:3; cf. 3:23,28-30). All these precautions were essential because **'The city was large and spacious, but there were few people in it, and the houses had not yet been rebuilt'** (7:4). Therefore, the citizens set up 'a vigilante style guard upon the city'.[2] Perhaps when

Nehemiah issued his orders concerning the protection of Jerusalem he was thinking of the mighty walls of Babylon which fell to the Persians.

Secondly, Nehemiah charged two men with the responsibility of affairs within the city: **'I put in charge of Jerusalem my brother Hanani, along with Hananiah the commander of the citadel'** (7:2). We read about Hanani, the first of these two men, in the opening chapter of Nehemiah. Hanani's visit to Babylon radically changed the life of his brother Nehemiah. We know very little, apart from this verse, about Hananiah, the second man chosen by Nehemiah. He may be the wall-builder who is mentioned in 3:30, and the citadel of which he was the commander was most likely 'the Tower of Hananel' (2:8; 3:1). Just as Nehemiah was on the lookout for the men to whom he could delegate the business of supervising Jerusalem, so office-bearers should encourage believers in whom they discern an aptitude for particular ministries in the church (2 Tim. 2:2).

It is clear from verse 2 that Nehemiah did not choose his brother out of favouritism, but because Hanani was competent for the rôle assigned to him. The Judean governor reports that his brother **'was a man of integrity and feared God more than most men do'**. His honesty was in marked contrast to the behaviour of the nobles, officials and governors who were reproved for exploiting their fellow-Jews (ch. 5) and the dignitaries in Jerusalem whose loyalties were divided (6:17-19). We have already discovered that the rich oppressed the poor because they did not fear God (5:9,15). Hanani's reverence for God was seen in the fact that he put himself to a great deal of trouble to inform Nehemiah about the desolate condition of the Jews in Jerusalem (ch. 1). Hanani was obviously a man who shared the compassion of Nehemiah for the Jews and one in whom they placed confidence as their representative. Nehemiah picked the right men for the job! These verses alert us to the need of caution in the choice of men and women for service in the local church. Personal holiness is more important than eloquence or gifts. A holy Christian with few talents can have a good influence in a neighbourhood and be useful in the work of God. Christians in positions of authority should excel in godliness.

The census (7:4-69)

Nehemiah tells us that as he was considering the best way to deal with the repopulation of Jerusalem, two things happened (7:5). Firstly, **'God put it into my heart to assemble the nobles, the officials and the common people for registration by families'**; secondly, **'I found the genealogical record of those who had been the first to return'** at the time of Zerubbabel, the same list as that preserved in Ezra 2. The discovery of the old register meant that Nehemiah could use it as the basis of his own enrolment and ensure that the new inhabitants of Jerusalem were descended from the original population. It is evident then that the purpose of this poll was 'to make sure of the city's continuity with the past'.[3]

A careful examination of the tables in Ezra 2 and Nehemiah 7 reveals minor differences which liberal theologians have seized on in an attempt to disprove the inerrancy of the Scriptures. One solution to these apparent discrepancies is offered by Coleman Luck: 'It has been suggested that the list in Ezra's book was prepared in Babylon of those who expected to return, while the one given by Nehemiah was made in Jerusalem itself of those who actually *did* return. This could account for the small variations.'[4] Another, and perhaps more feasible, answer to the problem is that the discrepancies are copyists' errors.

Why did God urge Nehemiah to make a census, and why

was the governor so concerned with these old records? It was critical that the genealogical archives should be well organized so that there would be no doubt, in years to come, that Jesus was the Messiah-King and that he came from the tribe of Judah as foretold by the ancient prophets (Gen. 49:10; Micah 5:2; see also Matt. 2:1-6; Heb. 7:14; Rev. 5:5).

The demand of God for holiness among his people is highlighted again in verses 64-65, where we read about the priests who **'searched for their family records, but they could not find them and so were excluded from the priesthood as unclean'**. A pure priesthood was vital if the Jews were to sustain a right relationship with the Lord. A corrupt priesthood would soon lead to a lowering of standards among the populace. The same is true today: once we are careless about whom we allow into our pulpits and elect as officers in the church, it will not be long before the whole church has drifted away from the principles of God's Word.

We have learnt from the books of Ezra and Nehemiah that the purity of the Jewish race and its separation from the surrounding wicked nations were to safeguard God's people from extinction as a distinct entity. The holiness of Old Testament believers was a preparation for the coming of the Lord Jesus Christ. The holiness of the church now prepares us for the second coming of Christ, the glorious King. The godliness of the church speeds the return of the Lord (2 Peter 3:10-14).

The support of the priests and temple workers (7:70-73)

'The heads of the families', who had been overshadowed by the rulers of the different cities, are now brought into prominence and commended for their contributions to God's work (7:70). Nehemiah joins these family heads in setting an example of ungrudging and cheerful giving to the treasury.

The 1,000 drachmas of gold (7:70) and the 20,000 drachmas of gold (7:71) weighed about nineteen pounds (8.5 kilograms) and about 375 pounds (170 kilograms) respectively. The 2,200 minas of silver (7:71) and the 2,000 minas of silver (7:72) came to about 1¼ tons (1.3 metric tons) and about 1 ton (1.1 metric tons) respectively.

There are two practical lessons which we may draw from these closing verses of Nehemiah 7. The first is that God's work is not to be supported by fund-raising efforts, but by the generous and sacrificial giving of the church. The other area of application in these verses is that Christians are to take seriously the financial support of those whom the Lord has called to serve him in a whole-time capacity. Paul makes the same point in his letter to the Christians of Galatia: 'Anyone who receives instruction in the word must share all good things with his instructor' (Gal. 6:6). This portion of Nehemiah 7 compels us to consider questions such as, 'Has the church to which I belong called an elder (or elders) to leave his secular employment for the benefit of the members? If so, are those members realistic in their financial support of the man and his family?'

This chapter of Nehemiah marks a transition from the building of the wall (chs 1-6) to the spiritual revitalizing of the nation (chs 8-10), which was followed by the final reforms of Nehemiah (chs 11-13).

20.
'The people of a book'

Please read Nehemiah 7:73 - 8:18

Try to imagine the scene presented to us in Nehemiah 8. It is Tisri, the seventh month of the sacred year (equivalent to our September-October), in the year 444 B.C., in the city of Jerusalem. Jews have travelled from all over Judah for a great assembly in the rebuilt capital city. A wooden platform has been erected in the large square at the Water Gate on the east side of the city. Ezra the priest, who retired from public life some thirteen years ago, steps on to the podium carrying a scroll. He begins the meeting with praise to God. As Ezra's eyes run over the throng he can see hands everywhere lifted up towards heaven and hears the united voices of the people crying out, 'Amen! Amen!' Soon the congregation are kneeling with their faces bowed down to the ground. Ezra opens the book and starts to read. The reading goes on and on and on from dawn to noon. And no one complains! They are eager to catch every word from the priest's lips. This assembly would be spoken about for years to come!

Listening to the book (7:73 - 8:12)

Now that the foundations of Jerusalem were relaid and its walls raised up, it was time for the nation itself to be re-established on the solid basis of God's Word. The two closely connected events of the completion of the walls and the reading of the Law occurred within the space of a few days (cf. 6:15 with 8:2; Elul was the sixth month and Tisri the seventh). The day described in Nehemiah 8 was 'to prove a turning point. From now on, the Jews would be predominantly "the people of a book".'[1] So today we are strong or weak depending on how closely we adhere to the inerrant Word of God.

It was the populace, rather than the leaders, who entreated Ezra **'to bring out the Book of the Law of Moses'** (8:1). This earnest request was no doubt the outcome of the faithful and persistent instruction of Ezra over many years, for 'Ezra had devoted himself to the study and observance of the Law of the Lord, and to teaching its decrees and laws in Israel' (Ezra 7:10). This thorough grounding in God's Word was exemplified in the godly lives of Ezra and Nehemiah. The inclination of the people to hear the law of God may also tie in with the rejection from the priesthood of those who 'searched for their family records, but they could not find them' (7:64). The exclusion of these men emphasized the demand of God for holiness as a prerequisite for worship and service. The Jews felt the need to know what God required of them, and such knowledge could only be gained from **'the Law of Moses, which the Lord commanded for Israel'** (8:1).

So Ezra walked out of obscurity and back into the limelight when he mounted the **'high wooden platform built for the occasion'**, alongside his thirteen assistants (8:4). Perhaps these men took turns with Ezra in reading from 'the Book of the Law'. The effect of these Levites supporting Ezra (8:4,7) was to make the point that those who wielded authority in the nation were themselves submissive to the law of God. He 'produced ... no new manifesto but the foundation articles of the faith ... these were credited with divine authority'.[2] When our church seems to make so little impact on the unconverted

while the charismatic church down the street is full every
Sunday, we face the temptation to alter our message or adapt
our methods to draw folk in. The *message* (God's Word) and
the *method* (the spread of God's Word through Christ-centred
preaching and God-glorifying evangelism) are ordained by
God and will therefore result in spiritual fruit.

Ezra the priest read the Scriptures **'aloud from daybreak
till noon'** (8:3). God's Word is too important to be read, or
preached, in an apathetic manner, or with a mumbling voice so
that the congregation are straining to hear. The way in which
Ezra read 'the Book of the Law' is instructive and so is the
location selected for this reading. The assembly gathered at
'the Water Gate' (8:1). The Word of God must be taken
where the people are so that it will be heard. We are to 'Go into
all the world and preach the good news to all creation,' rather
than waiting for the world to come to us! (Mark 16:15). When
we go we do so with the encouragement of God's promises,
such as Isaiah 55:10-11, ringing in our ears!

1. The people listened collectively

They gathered as a nation — **'All the people assembled'** (8:1)
— and as families — **'men and women and all who were
able to understand'** (8:2). Society as a whole benefits when
God's Word is honoured by a nation and by the families of that
nation. The wise man Solomon, Israel's third king, observed
that 'Righteousness exalts a nation, but sin is a disgrace to any
people' (Prov. 14:34). Our own country has drifted further and
further away from the Bible and consequently has lost much
of its greatness. The increase in crime, even among children,
and the breakdown of morality are instances of the disgrace
which sin brings to a nation. In such a climate we should take
seriously the injunction of Paul to pray for 'kings and all those
in authority' (1 Tim. 2:1-2).

It is imperative, especially in days when wickedness is rampant, that we bring up our children 'in the training and instruction of the Lord' (Eph. 6:4). The children were a significant part of this memorable convention (8:2). We ought not to underestimate the spiritual perception of children. There are many examples in the Bible (e.g. Josiah, 2 Kings 22-23) and in history of the conversion of children. It would appear that Isaac Watts, the well-known hymn-writer, was converted at a very young age.[3]

2. They listened unitedly

We read in verse 1 that **'All the people assembled as one man in the square before the Water Gate.'** These words are reminiscent of the words of Ezra 3:1, where we read of the Jews meeting 'as one man in Jerusalem' in the seventh month (the same month as the assembly in Nehemiah 8), to lay the foundation-stone of the temple in 537 B.C. Ezra was at the forefront of both assemblies. Their national identity was cemented as they joined as one to hear the law of God. True Christian unity is not based on subjective experiences but on the objective truth of God's Word.

3. They listened attentively

Nehemiah comments twice in chapter 8 on the attentiveness of the hearers. The Jews listened on the first day, from **'daybreak till noon'** (8:3), and then two weeks later at the Feast of Tabernacles (which began on the fifteenth day of the seventh month) **'day after day, from the first day to the last'** (8:18). 'The first day to the last' covered a seven-day period of time. They had an insatiable appetite for the Scriptures. Are we as zealous to hear the Word of God preached whenever we have the opportunity? Do we allow our thoughts to wander during the sermon rather than disciplining our minds to concentrate?

We read in verse 13 that **'the heads of all the families, along with the priests and the Levites'**, took the lead in hearing the words of the Law. Fathers in the home and spiritual leaders in the church should inculcate an eagerness for the Bible and preaching by their own example.

4. They listened reverently

Prayer and praise directed to **'the great God'** (8:6) prepared the hearts of the Jews to receive God's Word. Before Ezra read the Law he invoked God's blessing on those present. They responded with a fervent chorus of **'Amen! Amen!'**, which means, 'Yes, Lord, let it be.' The enthusiastic worshippers lifted up their hands towards heaven as a token of their utter dependence on God for his mercy. **'Then they bowed down and worshipped the Lord with their faces to the ground,'** an expression of their humility in the presence of the almighty God (8:6).

5. They listened intelligently

It is clear from verses 7 and 8 that the response of the Jews to the reading of the Law was not merely an outburst of mass hysteria, but rather their interaction with its message. As the second group of Levites moved among the people they carefully explained God's Word to them so that they could **'understand what was being read'** (8:8). Perhaps the large assembly broke up into smaller groups. The Bible is not a magic potion which will miraculously change us into saints regardless of our grasp of its doctrines. We can only implement the teaching of the Bible if we discern what that teaching demands of us. These Levites provide an excellent model for all who are involved in any kind of religious education. The outcome of this intelligent hearing of the Law was distress because of their failure to obey, followed by joy once they **'understood the words that had been made known to them'** (8:12). Another result was a readiness to make amends for their errant behaviour (8:13-18). Are we as quick to obey the Word of God?

6. They listened joyfully

The weeping of contrition preceded the rejoicing of pardon (8:9-10). Thomas Watson, a seventeenth-century Puritan pastor, remarked that he found two things difficult in his preaching: firstly, 'to make the wicked sad'; and secondly, 'to make the godly joyful'![14] The day of the assembly was **'sacred to the Lord'** (8:9); the occasion was solemn but not inhibiting, hence the command of Nehemiah to the congregation: **'Go and enjoy choice food and sweet drinks'** (8:10). Godliness and gloom are not inseparable twins!

Verses 9-12 remind me of an Anglican vicar's astonishment, when as a new convert, he discovered that Christians are meant to be happy: 'I can still remember my surprise when I first noticed the third line of the hymn "All people that on earth do dwell". In my hymn book the words quite clearly said "Him serve with mirth". My surprise was so great that I did not sing the rest of the hymn, but just stood there looking at the words. I had recently become a Christian and knew that many things in life would have to change. I had presumed that the happy things like laughter and joy would be among the first to receive drastic alterations.'[5]

The magnanimous Nehemiah (cf. 5:17-18) appeals to those who have plenty to share their food with the destitute **'who have nothing prepared'** (8:10). Nehemiah assures the Jews that **'The joy of the Lord is your strength'** (8:10). It gave

them strength to overcome their sense of guilt and to exult in
the grace of God towards them.

Living in booths (8:13-18)

The theme of joy forms a link between verses 9-12 and 13-18.
A look back to Deuteronomy 16:13-15 reveals that joy was a
feature of the Feast of Tabernacles. Moses commanded the
Israelites to 'Be joyful at your Feast... For seven days celebrate
the Feast ... and your joy will be complete.' Nehemiah tells us
that the joy of his contemporaries **'was very great'** because
they not only celebrated the deliverance of their fathers from
Egypt but also their own release from exile in Babylon (8:17).
The Feast of Tabernacles not only looked back to the
Exodus; it also reminded the Jews of the wandering of their
forefathers in the desert. We know from Ezra 3:4 that the Jews
who had returned from exile kept the Feast of Tabernacles, but
it is evident from Nehemiah 8 that the aspect of the festival that
involved the building of booths had been neglected. Now, in
obedience to the word of God through Moses (Lev. 23:33-44),
the Jews resolved to correct this oversight (8:14). Between the
second day of the assembly and the feast two weeks passed, in
which time the Jews collected the materials to erect booths and
spread the news about the forthcoming commemoration. Then
the people who lived in the city made their shelters on the flat
rooftops and the country folk constructed theirs in the court-
yards and streets of Jerusalem (8:14-16).
The Jews of Nehemiah's time kept this festival on a larger
scale than had been done since the time of Joshua, nearly 1,000
years earlier (8:17). The seven-day feast culminated in another
solemn assembly on the eighth day (8:18). Throughout the
Feast of Tabernacles **'Ezra read from the Book of the Law
of God'** (8:18). The **'regulation'** (8:18) refers to Deuteronomy

31:10-13, where Moses commanded the Law to be read every seven years at the Feast of Tabernacles. This may have been the seventh year, or Ezra may have been 'going beyond the minimum requirement of the law and introducing an annual reading ... but such became the custom in due course.'[6]

Kidner summarizes the effect of the proceedings recorded in Nehemiah 8: 'So the move to make the Scripture the guiding principle of Jewish life was powerfully initiated. The great teaching operation on the first day of the month, the training session which had followed it, and now the seven days of readings at the festival had exposed the people to the fundamentals of their faith with considerable thoroughness. But the clinching of it was yet to come, as the next two chapters will show.'[7]

21.
Amazing grace!

Please read Nehemiah chapter 9

Nehemiah's primary task in Judah was to complete the walls of Jerusalem (2:5). He had astonished his enemies, and his workforce, when he accomplished that goal in the short period of fifty-two days (6:15). Now we may have expected the Judean governor to pack his bags and return to his comfortable job as the cupbearer of Artaxerxes. In fact the opposite was true because Nehemiah was as concerned for the spiritual well-being of his fellow-Jews as he was for their physical welfare. Therefore he stayed put in Jerusalem, fully involved in the renewal and reforms of which we read in the closing chapters of his book.

As we move into Nehemiah chapter 9 we remind ourselves that a recurrent theme running through Ezra and Nehemiah is that the holy God desires a holy people to serve him. This is the reason why it was essential for the Jews in the past, and ourselves nowadays, to be 'the people of a book'. It is in that book, God's Word, that we ascertain how to please the Lord. We learn from Nehemiah 9 that the study of the Bible should lead to confession of sin. The consequence of confession of sin is a fresh realization of God's amazing grace.

Sorrow (9:1-4)

The Feast of Tabernacles, which lasted for seven days from 15 to 21 Tisri (September/October), was followed by an assembly on the eighth day (8:18). Then **'On the twenty-fourth day of the same month, the Israelites gathered together'** for a day of penitence (9:1). The intervening two days gave an opportunity for the congregation to adjust from joy to sorrow. This transition from praise to penitence was necessary if the Word of God was to have a lasting effect in the lives of God's people. The contrition of Nehemiah 9 was a prelude to the signing of the covenant of which we read in Nehemiah 10. It was a time for renewed dedication to God.

The intensity of the penitents' grief for their transgressions was given expression by **'fasting and wearing sackcloth and having dust on their heads'** (9:1). '"Fasting" was an act of self-denial that involved placing spiritual concerns over physical needs';[1] wearing sackcloth symbolized profound sorrow (Gen. 37:34; Jonah 3:3-5); dust on the head was a reminder of mortality: 'Dust you are and to dust you will return' (Gen. 3:19). Another token of the Jews' seriousness in seeking God was their separation **'from all foreigners'** (9:2), the worshippers of false gods who did not render obedience to Jehovah the true God. Separation from the non-Jewish nations was not a self-righteous 'holier-than-thou' attitude on the Jews' part, but compliance with God's command recorded in Leviticus 20:26: 'You are to be holy to me because I, the Lord, am holy, and I have set you apart from the nations to be my own.' The people of God rejected earthly comfort and some human friendships in their pursuit of God. The Lord Jesus Christ calls us to a life of self-denial. This does not mean that we become ascetics and despise all pleasure, or that we become hermits and shun all human company, but it does mean that we are serious in our quest for likeness to God.

The Jews' acknowledgement of their misdeeds embraced their own personal sins and those of their ancestors: **'They stood in their places and confessed their sins and the wickedness of their fathers'** (9:2). Parents not only pass on to their children a fallen nature but also act as rôle models of sinful conduct. Nevertheless God's grace can help us to break out of this spiral of wickedness so that we may, though still far from perfection, provide an example of godly living for future generations. The vehemence of the Jews' determination to leave their evil ways and consecrate themselves to God is seen in the fact that they stood for three hours — **'a quarter of the day'** — to hear **'the Book of the Law of the Lord their God'**, followed by a further three hours **'in confession and in worshipping the Lord their God'** (9:3). The contrition, like the earlier joy, was produced by the Word of God. And all this was prior to the petition of the Levites!

A survey of history (9:5-31)

It is evident from the words of verse 5, **'Blessed be your glorious name'**, that this survey of Israel's history was presented as a prayer to God. But God does not need a lesson in Jewish history, so what was the purpose of this résumé of historic events? It was an appeal to God, who in the past revealed himself as 'the great, mighty and awesome God, who keeps his covenant of love' (9:32), to display his power again on behalf of the chosen race in their present suffering. This narration of the former deeds of God was also a tonic to lift up the spirits of the Jews. Furthermore this survey was a warning to them not to rebel against God as their forefathers had done so often in the past. If we research church history lamenting the demise of 'the good old days' when chapels were full and preachers pulled the crowds, we shall sink into depression, but if we read of bygone days to discover how powerful God is and what he accomplished through his people, then we shall be encouraged as we serve him in our own generation.

Who prayed this prayer, which begins at verse 5 and goes through to verse 37? Some versions, for example the Revised Standard Version and the Amplified Bible, insert the statement, 'And Ezra said', at the beginning of verse 6. As the RSV footnote indicates these words are not found in the Hebrew text. The origin of the insertion is the Greek translation of the Old Testament known as the Septuagint. In the NIV verse 4 tells us that the Levites stood on the stairs and **'called with loud voices to the Lord their God'**. I think we must assume therefore that one of them prayed as the representative of the assembly. 'The Levites in verse 4 petitioned God voicing the distress of the people. The Levites in verse 5 praised God, leading the people in corporate worship.'[2] The **'stairs'** (8:4) may refer to the steps of the platform, or the steps which led from one courtyard of the temple to another.

The Levites focus on five facets of God's dealings with his people.

1. The glorious God who made the world (9:5-6)

The Levites began their invocation with adoration of Jehovah, the eternal and glorious Creator. There is no other god; he alone made the heavens and the earth. The Levites remind the Jews that this God had entered into a covenant relationship with Israel: **'Stand up and praise the Lord your God'**; therefore he would answer the plea of his people in their anguish and pardon all their sins. The worship of the Jews on earth mingled with the angels who are described as **'the multitudes of heaven'**.

2. *The righteous God who keeps his promises* (9:7-8)

The key to these two verses is found at the end of verse 8: **'You have kept your promise because you are righteous.'** This promise, given in the form of a solemn covenant, was that God would give to Abraham's posterity **'the land of the Canaanites'**. These words looked back to Genesis 12, which relates how God called Abraham, an occurrence already referred to in verse 7. The return of the Jews to Judah after seventy years in exile was proof that the faithful God had kept his oath made so long ago to Abraham.

We read in verse 7 that God did three things for Abraham: firstly, he chose him; secondly, he brought him from Ur (near the Persian Gulf in present-day Iraq) to Canaan (later called Israel); thirdly, he changed his name from Abram ('exalted father') to Abraham ('father of a multitude'). His old name may refer to his former status in Ur, whereas his new name predicted that he was to become the father of the Jewish race, and indeed the father of the church which is made up of converted Jews and Gentiles (Gen. 17:1-8).

The initial pledge which God made to Abraham concerning the land of Canaan was later expanded to include the descendants of Abraham, who would be more numerous than the sand on the beach and the stars in the sky (Gen. 13:14-17; 22:15-18). Wrapped up in these promises was one in which God spoke about Abraham's seed: 'Through your offspring all nations on earth will be blessed' (Gen. 22:18). The apostle Paul makes it clear in his letter to the Galatians that the offspring, or seed, of Abraham was Jesus Christ himself, through whom the gift of salvation came to sinners (Gal. 3:16). When Jesus, the Saviour of the world, came to earth and died on the cross the righteous God kept his promises to Abraham. These promises seemed a far cry from the experience of the Jews invoking the aid of God. However, the implication of the description of Abraham in verse 8, **'You found his heart faithful'**, is that only those who are unwavering in their devotion to God will know his favour. 'Obedience continues to be the passport to blessing.'³

3. The gracious God who cares for his people (9:9-15)

This section of the Levites' entreaty moves on from the time of the patriarch Abraham (the twenty-second century B.C.) to the days of Moses (the fifteenth century B.C.).⁴ The God enthroned in heaven was not too far away to see the suffering of the slaves in Egypt (9:9). In the book of Exodus Moses comments several times on God's care for the afflicted Jews. There is an illustration of this is in the first chapter, where we read of Pharaoh's complaint that the Hebrew population was still growing in spite of his order that the male babies should be killed at birth. Moses sees in the fact that the angry king did not harm the midwives an expression of God's goodness: 'So God was kind to the midwives and the people increased and became even more numerous' (Exod. 1:20; cf. 2:23-25). The caring Lord sent Moses to Pharaoh to demand the release of the slaves. When the king refused to comply with God's command through Moses, the Lord **'sent miraculous signs and wonders against Pharaoh'**. The plagues demonstrated the superior power of God and punished the Egyptian tyrant for his arrogance (9:10).

The Levites' recollection, **'You made a name for yourself'** (9:10), reminds us that the magicians of Egypt were compelled to acknowledge after the plague of gnats: 'This is the finger of God.' Tragically Pharaoh did not repent because his 'heart was hard and he would not listen' (Exod. 8:19). When eventually the stubborn monarch freed the captives he soon regretted his decision and chased them to the Red Sea, where their cry of desperation was heard by the mightier

Sovereign than Pharaoh (9:9). God displayed his extraordinary strength as he **'divided the sea before them'** and **'hurled their pursuers into the depths, like a stone into mighty waters'** (9:11).

The Jews left Egypt to spend forty years in the wilderness. During those long weary years their loving heavenly Father was their guide, defender and provider (9:12,15,21). Like a wise father he not only looked after their welfare, but he also gave them rules for the maintenance of true religion and to uphold justice and morality, plus regulations to promote good health in a close-knit nomad community (9:13). These **'regulations and laws ... decrees and commands'** and the weekly Sabbath for rest and worship (9:14) constituted the Jews as a theocracy — a nation ruled by God. This God, who exhibited his mercy and his might to his own people in the Exodus and throughout the desert journey, would not ignore the plight of those who complained, 'We are slaves today, slaves in the land you gave our forefathers' (9:36). The God whose heart was touched at the pain of the oppressed Hebrews in Egypt and who watched over them in the wasteland watches over us. One day we shall see Satan, a worse enemy than Pharaoh, crushed under our feet (Rom. 16:20).

4. The compassionate God who does not abandon his people (9:16-26)

There is a striking contrast drawn in this section between the ungrateful Jews and the indulgent God. The Levites did not mince their words in their delineation of their own race. For example, **'Our forefathers became arrogant and stiffnecked, and did not obey your commands. They refused to listen and failed to remember the miracles you performed among them'** (9:16-17). They were so rebellious that they **'appointed a leader in order to return to their**

slavery' (9:17), and worshipped the golden calf while Moses was enjoying fellowship with God (9:18). The people who were taught to hallow God's name **'committed awful blasphemies'** (9:18,26). Afterwards God gave the Jews the military prowess to possess the land of Canaan and drive out its inhabitants. What was their response? They not only put God's law out of sight, behind their backs, but also killed the prophets who insisted on preaching God's message to them (9:26).

Surely God would wipe his hands of this incorrigible race? Nothing could be further from the truth! We read, **'You did not desert them, even when they cast for themselves an image of a calf'** (9:17-18; cf. 9:19). Verses 19-21 contain indisputable proof that God did not forsake the Jews, in spite of their rebellious behaviour. He not only continued to guide them and provide their every need in an inhospitable environment, he also sent his **'good Spirit to instruct them'** (9:20). It was the Holy Spirit who equipped Moses to teach and lead the Israelites. Later the Spirit spoke through the prophets, men like Isaiah and Jeremiah, to admonish the Jews who persisted in their disobedience of God (9:30). The same Spirit was active in the ministries of Ezra, his fellow priests and Nehemiah the Judean governor. We often overlook the work of the Holy Spirit prior to his descent on the Day of Pentecost.

The cause of the Lord's refusal to abandon his people was his mercy. Fourteen days prior to the events of Nehemiah 9, on 10 Tisri, the Jews celebrated the annual Day of Atonement on which two goats were slain in the place of transgressors. This demonstration of the Lord's kindness pointed forward to Christ, the Lamb of God who died for sinners (Lev. 16; John 1:29). Verse 17 is an exhilarating verse when we are burdened with the guilt of our sin: **'But you are a forgiving God, gracious and compassionate, slow to anger and abounding in love.'** The emphasis of these words is that God would cease to be God if he did not pardon repentant sinners. The term 'compassionate' 'has overtones of the warm, passionate feeling a mother has for her child'.⁵ The meaning of 'slow to anger and abounding in love' is that God is reluctant to discipline covenant-breakers, thus giving them time to repent, but is quick to fulfil his own covenant obligations. We too, like the Jews of Nehemiah's time, may come to this benign God with all our sins and all our sorrows! He is the God of amazing grace!

5. The sovereign God who achieves his plans (9:27-31)

There was an implied warning in the Levites' recounting of the Jews' earlier misdemeanours. Even the forbearing God comes to an end of patience with obdurate offenders. Therefore the Lord **'handed them over to their enemies, who oppressed them'**. This happened time and again, but each time, **'When they were oppressed they cried out to you. From heaven you heard them, and in your great compassion you gave them deliverers, who rescued them from the hand of their enemies'** (9:27). The 'deliverers' were the judges, such as Deborah, Gideon and Samson. Though God **'abandoned them to the hand of their enemies'** (9:28), it was only a temporary abandonment. **'But in your great mercy you did not put an end to them or abandon them, for you are a gracious and merciful God'** (9:31). These times of God 'handing over' his people to their foes reached a climax in the seventy years of exile in Babylon, which ended when 'The Lord moved the heart of Cyrus king of Persia' to allow the Jews to return back to their homeland in Israel (Ezra 1:1). It was the descendants of those migrants who were now pleading with the same benevolent God for his assistance.

Through all the cycles of backsliding and subsequent repentance the sovereign God was working according to his precise and perfect timetable. The waywardness of his own people and the depravity of their adversaries could not thwart his decrees. He would allow no one, nor any world power, however powerful, to destroy the nation which he singled out to be the vehicle through which he would reveal himself to the world. Every event was leading on to the birth of his beloved Son at Bethlehem and his atoning death at Calvary.

Supplication (9:32-38)

In this peroration to their petition, the Levites contemplate the nature of God, who is **'great, mighty and awesome ... who keeps his covenant of love'** (9:32). The preceding overview of Israel's history establishes beyond any doubt that God is indeed 'great, mighty and awesome'. In the presence of this God the Jews hung their heads in shame as they declared, **'In all that has happened to us, you have been just; you have acted faithfully, while we did wrong'** (9:33). From the king downwards, the nation **'did not pay attention to your commands or the warnings you gave them'** (9:34). Even while enjoying the material blessings of God, **'They did not serve you or turn from their evil ways'** (9:35). Their present hardship (9:32) and servitude to the Persian king were directly related to their insubordination to God (9:36-37). The sincerity of the Jews was seen in their new commitment of themselves to God (9:38). The God of amazing grace has promised in his Word to respond to this kind of frank and open confession of sin. When we feel the weight of sin on our consciences we would do well to reflect on God's promises to forgive our sins found in passages such as 1 John 1:9.

22.
The covenanters

Please read Nehemiah 9:38 - 10:39

'If we are tempted to think of the Books of Ezra and Nehemiah as unattractively exclusivist, we may reflect that the separation of Judah *from* the peoples was part of a plan of God which was ultimately *for* the peoples.'[1] This comment of McConville's on Nehemiah 10:28 stresses a very important principle which we ought to bear in mind as we read this passage. We are reminded yet again that the Lord Jesus Christ, born within the confines of the Jewish race, brought salvation for all the peoples of the world. Just as the separation of the Jewish nation brought benefit to all races, so the Christian church must remain a distinct entity to declare God's message to the unconverted.

The preparation for signing the covenant (9:38)

The final verse of Nehemiah 9, which is the first verse of chapter 10 in the Hebrew Bible, forms the bridge between the plea for pardon and the oath of allegiance. **'In view of all this'**, directs our thoughts back to the reading of 'the Book of the Law' (ch. 8) and the prayer of confession (ch. 9), which prepared the hearts of the Jews to enter into a solemn contract with their God. Both the reading and the prayer caused them to realize how far they had fallen short of God's requirements. However, they were not in despair, since they had grasped that the God who disciplined them because of their sins was ready to forgive them because of his mercy. Therefore the people of God determined to make a written **'binding agreement'**, signed and sealed by **'our leaders, our Levites and our priests'**. The seal affixed to the formal document authenticated the agreement.

Another link with the earlier part of chapter 9 is found in the Hebrew word translated in verse 38 as 'agreement'. It is not the usual one used for covenant throughout chapter 10, but a word indicating an act of faithfulness — the kind of faithfulness for which Abraham was distinguished: 'You found his heart faithful to you' (9:8). The 'binding agreement' of the Jews was an affirmation of loyalty to the Lord. Adherence to this pact would establish that they were indeed the true children of Abraham.[2]

The people who signed the covenant (10:1-29)

1. Nehemiah the governor and Zedekiah (10:1)

Nehemiah, who kept a low profile throughout the spiritual renewal outlined in the previous two chapters of his memoirs, now takes the lead in signing the covenant. It is generally agreed among the commentators that Zedekiah was one of the civil leaders rather than one of the priests enumerated in the following seven verses. The reason behind this view is that 'Legal documents were normally attested by a scribe and witnesses, with an important official's secretary signing in the second place.'[3] It would appear that Zedekiah was the personal secretary of Nehemiah the governor.

2. *The priests* (10:2-8)

When we compare these verses with chapter 12:12-21 we
realize that the names of the twenty-one priests are family
names. The head of each priestly family could sign the
covenant on behalf of his family in much the same way as I
acted as the representative of my brothers and sister as the
executor of my mother's will. It is also informative to put these
two passages in Nehemiah alongside Ezra 7:1, where we read
that Seraiah, who is mentioned in both references, was the
father of Ezra. This is the reason why Ezra did not sign the
agreement for himself. His father signed it for Ezra and the rest
of his family.

3. *The Levites* (10:9-13)

Some of these seventeen names are familiar: for example,
Sherebiah and Hashabiah travelled with Ezra from Babylon to
Jerusalem (Ezra 8:18-19), and at least six of these men assisted
Ezra in reading the law (8:7).

4. *The leaders of the people* (10:14-27)

This list, like that of the priests, names the heads of the families
represented. The first part of it, **'Parosh ... Magpiash'** (10:14-
20a) resembles, with a few variations, the register in Ezra 2:3-
30, whereas the second part, **'Meshullam ... Baanah'**
(10:20b-27) is similar to the roll of wall-builders in Nehemiah
3. 'Not all the names included in Ezra 2 and Nehemiah 7
appear in this list [Nehemiah 10]. Apparently some family
names had passed out of existence. The additional names may
represent recent arrivals to Judah.'[4]

5. The rest of the people (10:28-29)

Finally **'the rest of the people'** added their support to the governor, priests, Levites and leaders, thus signifying their recognition of their obligations in the covenant. Nehemiah remarks on three features of this fifth group.

Firstly, *they were loyal to God*. They **'separated themselves from the neighbouring peoples'** (10:28). This was vital for the maintenance of the true worship of God and to make him known to the idol-worshipping countries which surrounded the land of Judah. The practical outcome of this separation was the promise not to allow their daughters to marry non-Jews (10:30), and their refusal to engage in trading on the Sabbath with foreign merchants (10:31). The separated Jews kept the Sabbath as a day separated from other days in order to praise God.

Secondly, *they loved God's Word*. This was the cause of the Jews' devotion to God. They **'separated themselves ... for the sake of the Law of God'** (10:28). Their acceptance of the covenant was an avowal of their submission to the authority of the Word of God. So serious was their commitment to the Lord and his Word that they **'[bound] themselves with a curse and an oath to follow the Law of God given through Moses the servant of God'**. They confessed that they deserved punishment, and that God would be just to inflict it if they broke their vows. The thought of verse 29 is derived from Deuteronomy 28, where Moses taught the Hebrews that blessing would be the reward of obedience and that the curse of God would fall on those who disobeyed the divine commands.

Four synonyms are used in verse 29 which highlight various aspects of our interaction with God's Word. The different shades of meaning of these terms, according to Laney,[5] are as follows: **'the Law'** denotes instructions from the Lord, and **'the commands'** refer to God's rules, whereas the **'regulations'** indicate the judicial decisions of the Lord. The fourth word, **'decrees'**, is used of standards of conduct which are permanent. This word comes from a root which means 'to engrave'. The Scriptures are not merely to be learnt by rote, though Bible memorization is commendable; they are to be engraved on the heart.

Thirdly, *they all affirmed their allegiance to the Lord.* The men, along with their **'wives and all their sons and daughters who are able to understand — all these now join their brothers the nobles, and bind themselves ... to follow the Law of God'** (10:28-29). From the nobles down to the most humble, male and female, adults and children — all signed the covenant. It is interesting to note that the children old enough to understand were not excluded. Are we sometimes too slow to accept a child's profession of salvation and a little hesitant (if we are Baptists) to baptize believing children? Perhaps our behaviour may on occasions be similar to that of the disciples who pushed the infants away from Jesus, the Friend of children (Mark 10:13-16).

The promises of the covenant (10:30-39)

The Jews did not talk vaguely about compliance with God's law; rather they pledged themselves to obedience in certain specified areas of their corporate life as the people of God.

1. Mixed marriages (10:30)

The Jews promised **'not to give our daughters in marriage to the peoples around us or take their daughters for our sons'** (10:30). The prohibition of marriage to men and women of other ethnic groups was not racial discrimination but a religious injunction. The necessity for this stance was clearly explained when the Lord gave Moses, at Sinai, the tablets of stone containing the law. Intermarriage with the non-Jewish races would soon lead to the worship of their gods. The veneration of idols was regarded as unfaithfulness to God, who had chosen Israel to be his bride: 'Do not worship any other god, for the Lord, whose name is Jealous, is a jealous God' (Exod. 34:12-17). People born outside of the Jewish religion who turned in repentance and faith to Jehovah were welcomed by him and his chosen race. An example of this is found in Ezra 6:20-21.

It is illuminating to consider the approach of the Jews to the Mosaic law. A pedantic Jew could have argued that Moses only forbad marriage to 'the Amorites, Canaanites, Hittities, Perizzites, Hivites and Jebusites' — names which bore little relationship to the population of Judah in the fifth century B.C. The Jews entered into the spirit of the commandment when they used the all-embracing terminology, **'the peoples around us'** (10:30). We may learn from this how to interpret the many intricate laws contained in the Pentateuch. We must get at the principle behind regulations such as those concerning infectious skin diseases (Lev. 13:1-46), or directives like 'Do not wear clothes of wool and linen woven together' (Deut. 22:11). Though we believe in the verbal inspiration of the Scriptures we obviously cannot interpret everything in a strictly literal manner, no more than the Jews did at the time of Nehemiah.

As we read about the momentous contract which the Jews made with God we may be surprised to discover that not long afterwards, when Nehemiah was away in Persia, some 'men of Judah ... married women from Ashdod, Ammon and Moab' (13:23). Why did the Jews find it so hard to resist the allurement of marriage to non-Jewish spouses and the adoption of their gods? Segregation undoubtedly led to misunderstanding and even to confrontation. It was easier to live at peace with neighbouring races and ignore their wicked conduct. It may be that the pagan families could offer riches and social standing. We ought not to be too quick to condemn these Jews. Sometimes Christians have lived by this policy of 'Anything for a quiet life' or 'Peace at any price'. Have we always been true to God since the time of our conversion to him?

2. *The Sabbath* (10:31)

The Jews' second undertaking was not to buy merchandise on the Sabbath day from the traders who later swarmed into the rebuilt capital city (13:15-22). A Jew, intent on Sabbath trading, could of course argue that God's command was not infringed because he was not actually working when buying from a foreign salesman. As with the precepts concerning marriage, the people of God were more concerned with the meaning of the fourth commandment rather than the letter of the law. Though as Christians we do not observe a seventh-day Sabbath, nevertheless we do enter into the purport of the fourth commandment when we keep one day in seven as a special day for the adoration of God. As Christians we meet on Sunday, rather than Saturday, in commemoration of Christ's resurrection on the first day of the week. We read in Nehemiah 13 that the Jews went back on their promises concerning the Sabbath. Old sins, like weeds, will spring up again if we are not vigilant.

Every seventh year was observed as a year-long sabbath when the land was left fallow according to the instructions given by God to Moses: 'For six years you are to sow your fields and harvest the crops, but during the seventh year let the land lie unploughed and unused. Then the poor among your people may get food from it, and the wild animals may eat what they leave...' (Exod. 23:10-11). Obedience to God would not bring starvation because of his bounty in the sixth year: 'I will send you such a blessing in the sixth year that the land will yield enough for three years' (Lev. 25:1-7,20-22).

Moreover, in the seventh year the Jews promised, **'We ... will cancel all debts.'** This again was a provision which the generous God made for the poor (Deut. 15:1-11). Jesus encapsulated the teaching of these passages in his Sermon on the Mount: 'Blessed are the merciful, for they will be shown mercy' (Matt. 5:7).

3. Provision relating to worship in the temple (10:32-39)

The theme of the closing segment of Nehemiah 10 is found in the last verse: **'We will not neglect the house of our God.'** The worship of God was at the centre of their lives and was the reason for their existence as a unique nation set apart from all other nations. Therefore everything concerning worship, even down to the mundane chore of providing firewood for the sacrifices, was carefully planned (10:34). Some time later Nehemiah returned to Persia. When he came back again to Jerusalem he was distressed at the laxity of the leaders concerning the temple. 'So I rebuked the officials and asked them, "Why is the house of God neglected?"' (13:11). How soon our good intentions are forgotten!

These verses teach us about the importance of systematic giving for the support of the Lord's work and of those who serve on behalf of the church. It is clear from verses 32-33 that our giving is to continue in times of recession; it is then that the need of our stewardship is greater than ever. The law required that when a census was taken everyone over twenty years of age was obliged to donate half a shekel (about 6 grams) to maintain the worship of God (Exod. 30:11-16). The Jews assume this responsibility, though at a reduced rate of **'a third of a shekel'** (about 4 grams), presumably because of economic conditions. These verses do not provide us with an excuse to reduce our collections when we are in financial difficulties. Verses 34-39 reveal that the Jews were contributing far in excess of their 'third of a shekel' for the upkeep of the temple. What they lacked in hard cash was given in kind. When money is short we ought to decrease our expenditure on leisure pursuits rather than cut back on our donations to the Lord's work.

Verse 36 refers back to the deliverance of the Jews from bondage in Egypt. Israel was the first-born son of God; therefore Pharaoh's refusal to release the Jews was punished by the death of his first-born son and all the other first-born sons of Egyptian families (Exod. 4:22). When we read Exodus 12 we learn that this death sentence was not restricted to the men but also included animals. The Jewish first-born sons were spared when the angel of death saw the blood of the paschal lamb spread on the doorposts (Exod. 12:12-13). Once in the promised land the Jews were to thank God for their deliverance by giving to him 'the first offspring of every womb' — livestock and human. However, the first-born son was spared from death by the sacrifice of an animal slain as a substitute (Exod. 13:11-16). The relevance of verse 36 to believers is contained in passages such as Romans 12:1-2 and 1 Corinthians 6:19-20. We may sum up the application of Nehemiah 10:36 to ourselves as follows: God is the Master whom we obey and Jesus is the Saviour whom we love.

23.
Praise the Lord for volunteers!

Please read Nehemiah chapter 11

The building of the city walls (chs 1-6) and the spiritual renewal of God's people (chs 8-10) were accompanied by the formation of a new fraternity within Jerusalem (chs 7; 11; 12). In chapter 11 Nehemiah returns again to the problem of how to repopulate the capital city of Jerusalem in order to decrease its vulnerability to enemy attack. The defence of the capital was vital because within its walls was the temple around which Jewish life and worship centred.

An integral part of the repopulation of Jerusalem was the census of the nation (ch. 7), which ensured that the residents of the city were of unmixed Jewish descent. This concern for a pure clan was not a racist policy but was crucial to safeguard the exclusive worship of God and the distinct identity of his own people. It was fitting that a 'a holy nation' (Exod. 19:6) should live in **'the holy city'** (11:1,18). Both citizens and city belonged to God. The members of the city of God's church are 'called to be saints' (Rom. 1:7). Does our conduct match our title? Do we live up to what God requires of us?

Leaders (11:1)

The Jews were not a 'rabble of refugees, settling down anywhere',¹ but a well-organized community with wise and mature overseers serving under the direction of Nehemiah the governor. In addition to Hanani and Hananiah (7:2), the two leaders appointed at the time of the census, several chief officers were given responsibility for the various groups within Jerusalem. Joel and Judah supervised the Benjamites (11:9), Zabdiel was **'the chief officer'** for the priests (11:14) and Uzzi directed the Levites (11:22). We do not read that Hanani and Hananiah felt threatened by the new leaders or that they found it difficult to co-operate with them. They all worked together for the common good of God's people. Whatever rôle we fulfil in the church, we ought to be more concerned with the glory of God than with our own reputation or prestige.

Volunteers (11:1-2)

Once **'the leaders of the people'** had settled in Jerusalem, Nehemiah took steps to encourage a tenth of the inhabitants of the towns of Judah to uproot themselves, with their families, to move into the capital city. This ratio of one person to every nine was arrived at through the casting of lots throughout the towns and villages of Judah (11:1). This method insured impartiality, thus removing any cause for complaint.

We often read in the Old Testament about the casting of lots to determine the will of God. Another incident of drawing lots is given in Nehemiah 10:34 and relates to the provision of wood for the temple sacrifices. It is evident from Proverbs 16:33 that the use of lots in the Old Testament era showed the Jews' trust in God, 'The lot is cast into the lap, but its every decision is from the Lord.' When we turn to the New Testament we discover only one reference to the use of lots and that occurred before the descent of the Holy Spirit at Pentecost

(Acts 1:26). Is it wrong for Christians to cast lots for guidance from God? We are in a better position to discern the Lord's will than the people of God in Bible days. We now have the more widespread ministry of the Spirit plus the completed canon of Scripture. Therefore we are to direct our lives by the guidelines for godly living which God gives to us in his Word.

We read in verse 2 that **'The people commended all the men who volunteered to live in Jerusalem.'** It is not clear if these men were additional to those selected by ballot, or the same group. However we understand this verse, we cannot escape its emphasis on the willingness of these men to sacrifice their own interests and comforts for the benefit of their race. This self-denial was more than patriotism: it was the overflow of their devotion to God himself. Those who previously contributed a tenth of their produce and possessions to sustain the worship in the temple (10:37-39) now gave a tenth of their men to guard the city in which that temple was situated. The chosen tenth did not grumble that the lot fell on them, but rather gave themselves ungrudgingly as an offering to the Lord.

Many years later the apostle Paul commented on this same kind of dedication from the family of Stephanas, 'the first converts in Achaia', who 'devoted themselves to the service of the saints' (1 Cor. 16:15). In his second letter to the church in Corinth Paul mentioned the generous members of the Macedonian churches who 'gave themselves first to the Lord and then to us' (2 Cor. 8:5). Do we show this sort of commitment to the Lord and to his people? Are we as ready to respond when asked by fellow church members to undertake some work on their behalf?

The commendation of the volunteers may echo the song of Deborah, in which God was praised for volunteers in the fight against Jabin, the King of Canaan:

When the princes in Israel take the lead,
  when the people willingly offer themselves—
  praise the Lord!

(Judg. 5:2).

It is disheartening when Christians have to be cajoled into service, but it fills the church with praise when they volunteer!

The urban population (11:3-24)

1. The tribes of Judah and Benjamin (11:3-9)

The new residents of Jerusalem were drawn from a cross-section of people who lived in the towns of Judah (11:3). The occupants of 'the holy city' belonged mostly, though not exclusively, to the tribes of Judah, Benjamin and Levi. These tribes 'had stayed with David's heirs, to form the kingdom of Judah when the rest had broken away; now the future of Israel lay with them and with those who had rallied to them from the other tribes'.[2] It was the tribes of Benjamin and Judah, with the priests and Levites, that returned from exile under the leadership of Zerubbabel (Ezra 1:5).

The three tribes of Benjamin, Judah and Levi were joined by those of Ephraim and Manasseh, the descendants of Joseph's two sons (1 Chron. 9:1-3; Gen. 46:20). Judah was held in high esteem among the other tribes, whereas the smaller clan of Benjamin was known for its ferocious courage and mastery in war (Gen. 49:8,27). How could the families from these two tribes live peacefully in the restricted confines of Jerusalem? They were able to do so because of their common goal to see the city populated and the worship of God maintained. Likewise, in the church converts often come from widely differing backgrounds and may sometimes have clashing personalities. Christ, who united by his death the warring factions of Jews and Gentiles, enables us to live in harmony with one another. His love poured into our hearts becomes the cement which binds us together. This is a theme which the apostle Paul develops in his letter to the Ephesians (Eph. 2:11-22).

In verse 4 Nehemiah writes about **'a descendant of Perez'**. 1 Chronicles 9:6 also lists the descendants of Perez's twin brother, Zerah. Perez and Zerah were the sons of Judah. They were born as the result of Tamar, the widowed daughter-in-law of Judah, pretending to be a prostitute, in order to get him to fulfil a broken promise. The sordid story is told in Genesis 38. It was the descendants of these twins, born in such tragic circumstances, who cheerfully resettled in the city of Jerusalem. Grace overcame disgrace! Matthew, the Gospel writer, includes Perez in his family tree of Jesus Christ, the friend of sinners (Matt. 1:3). God has the power to bring good out of evil. He can save those who have come from homes of deprivation and depravity so as to display the beauty of his grace in their lives.

There is a further link with the story of Judah and Tamar at the end of verse 5, where there is mention of **'a descendant of Shelah'**. Shelah was the third son of Judah, by the Canaanite Shua. Tamar married Er, Judah's first-born, whose wickedness was punished with death. Tamar was promised that she could marry Shelah when he grew older. This promise was never kept; hence the deception of Tamar which led to the births of Perez and Zerah (Gen. 38:1-7,11,26).

Another interesting point to note about the 468 descendants of Perez is that Nehemiah describes them as **'able men'** (11:6), translated as 'valiant' in the AV. Further on he portrays some of the priests as **'able men'** whose **'chief officer was Zabdiel son of Haggedolim'** (11:14). The name 'Haggedolim' means 'the great'. It was essential to have men of ability to re-establish the civic and spiritual life of Jerusalem. The Hebrew word for 'able', which can indicate wealth, strength or ability, is used in Ruth 2:1, where Boaz, the future husband of Ruth, is called 'a man of standing'. He was respected and loved by all who were acquainted with him. Boaz was descended from Perez, the son of Judah (Ruth 4:18-22; Matt. 1:3-6).

Nehemiah totals the descendants of Benjamin as 928 in verse 8, whereas the compiler of the Chronicles numbers them as 956 (1 Chron. 9:9). There is also a difference in the numbering of the gatekeepers. Is the correct figure 212 (1 Chron. 9:22) or 172 (Neh. 11:19)? How do we account for these discrepancies? The difference in the tally of gatekeepers may easily be explained. Some of their relatives who lived in the towns around Jerusalem were part-time gatekeepers who came into the city for a week's duty at a time (1 Chron. 9:25). I have not yet uncovered a satisfactory solution to account for the apparent contradiction between the two figures for the descendants of Benjamin. There can be no doubt that every word of Scripture is God-breathed (2 Tim. 3:16), but sometimes we have to suspend judgement until more information is available to us. Over the years archaeology has thrown a great deal of light on the customs and culture of the ancient nations referred to in the Old Testament, and may in the future help us to resolve this conundrum.

2. *The priests* (11:10-14)

The priests, a smaller group within the tribe of Levi, were descended from Aaron, the first high priest and the brother of Moses. These priests were responsible for the offering of the sacrifices and the maintenance of the ritual as prescribed in the law of Moses. The priests, as the religious leaders of the nation, exerted great power over the people. One of the priests not listed in chapter 11 was Eliashib, who was 'closely associated with Tobiah' (13:4) and a relative of Sanballat (13:28); therefore he was disloyal to Nehemiah the governor. The fact that Tobiah was allowed the use of a large room in the temple suggests that some of the other priests sided with Eliashib rather than supporting the reforms of Nehemiah. Though we must not infer too much from the silence of Scripture it does appear that none of the priests protested against this misuse of God's house (13:4-5). The priests were in a position to cause agitation and dissatisfaction among the people with the leaders designated by Nehemiah.

3. The Levites (11:15-24)

The Levites were the support team for the priests so that the worship of God in the temple ran smoothly. Nehemiah tells us that these Levites **'had charge of the outside work of the house of God'** (11:16) — they kept the exterior of the temple in good repair. Two groups of Levites are specifically mentioned by Nehemiah: the gatekeepers (11:19) and the singers (11:22-23). We learn about the gatekeepers' activities when we turn to 1 Chronicles 9:17-34. These men not only opened and closed the temple doors, but also provided round-the-clock security for the sanctuary. Some were responsible for the upkeep of the rooms and the safety of the treasures; others were entrusted with the utensils and the care of the furnishings, oil, incense and spices. There were priests who mixed the spices and a Levite who baked the offering bread, while the Kohathites (descended from Kohath, son of Jacob's son Levi) prepared 'for every Sabbath the bread set out on the table'.

The second group singled out by Nehemiah were the singers. The leader of the temple choir was **'Uzzi ... one of Asaph's descendants'**. Asaph, who wrote some of the Psalms,[3] was one of the musicians who played when the Ark of the Covenant was brought into Solomon's temple (2 Chron.

5:12). He was among the Levites 'put in charge of the music' in the tabernacle by King David, father of Solomon (1 Chron. 6:31,39). The singers were carefully supervised and their duties **'regulated'** (11:23). We assume that **'Mattaniah ... the director who led in thanksgiving and prayer'** (11:17), arranged the worship in consultation with Uzzi, the temple choir-master. These singers were at the forefront of the festivities for the dedication of the Jerusalem walls (12:27-43).

We learn from these verses (11:17,22-23) that for the Jews, 'Worship was too important to leave unplanned.'[4] Are we sometimes too casual in our approach to worship? Does our emphasis on preaching mean that we do not give enough serious thought to the adoration of God? For example, do we select hymns or choruses because of their lively tunes, or because of the sentiments which they express? Of course there is no reason why we should sing excellent hymns to dull tunes! It can be rather like walking a tightrope to ensure the right balance between joyfulness and reverence in our veneration of God.

King Artaxerxes, who took a personal interest in the Jews, showed a special concern for the ministry of the temple singers (11:23). A man named Pethahiah, from the tribe of Judah, was commissioned to send regular dispatches to Artaxerxes and to advise the Persian monarch on matters relating to the Jews (11:24).

4. The temple servants (11:21)

The gatekeepers and singers were aided by the temple servants, who **'lived on the hill of Ophel'**, which led up to the temple at the north end of Jerusalem. These temple servants were 'a body that David and the officials had established to assist the Levites' (Ezra 8:20). The Authorized Version retains the Hebrew name for these men, 'the Nethinims', which means 'the dedicated ones', and is reminiscent of the description of the Levites given in Numbers 8:16: 'They are the Israelites who are to be given wholly to me.' They may, like the Gibeonites, have been non-Jews who served the people of God (Josh. 9:27).

The rural community (11:25-36)[5]

The Persian province of Judah shared boundaries with Samaria in the north and Idumea (Edom) in the south. However, many of the **'villages with their fields'**, or farms (11:25), enumerated in Nehemiah's catalogue were outside of the geographical area of Judah. For example, **'Kiriath Arba'** (11:25), another name for Hebron (Josh. 14:15), was about twenty miles south of Jerusalem and **'Beersheba'** (11:30), two miles east of the modern town of the same name, was even further away from the capital city; both places were in the land of Idumea. The villages mentioned in verses 34-35, including Ono (to which Nehemiah was invited for a dialogue with Sanballat, 6:1-2), were about thirty miles north-west of Jerusalem. As citizens of Persia the people were allowed to set up home wherever they wanted, which meant that the Jews could move to the towns or cities where their families formerly lived. The expression, **'So they were living ...'** (11:30) may suggest that the people of God were tolerated rather than welcomed. The Jews felt like slaves in the land given to them by God himself (9:36-37). **'The Valley of the Craftsmen'** (11:35) was not far from Joppa, the nearest port to Jerusalem for unloading timber from Lebanon (Ezra 3:7); it was therefore the most suitable location for these artisans.

The presence of **'the priests and Levites ... in all the towns of Judah'** (11:20) and the locating of **'some of the divisions of the Levites ... in Benjamin'** (11:36) were essential for the teaching of God's Word in all the Jewish territories. The Word of God, then and now, is needed in the urban cities as well as in the rural towns and villages. The revelation of God, and the adoration of God as a result of that knowledge, was the sole reason for the Jews' existence as a nation and for the protection of that race by God. It is through the Jew, Jesus Christ, that we enter into fellowship with the Lord and can offer to him spiritual worship (John 17:3; 4:21-26).

24.
Songs of praise

Please read Nehemiah chapter 12

Walking round an old cemetery would be dismissed as morbid and boring by some people, but to the person who is tracing his ancestors, or to the member of a local history society, it can be fascinating! Similarly a study of the first twenty-six verses of Nehemiah 12 may seem as if we are reading the names on the gravestones of long-forgotten people, or it may be a stimulus to labour for God with renewed devotion. It all depends on our viewpoint. The story of the church is more extensive than the achievements of outstanding people and major events: it consists of a vast number of men and women whose names are no longer remembered but who, like David, 'served God's purpose' in their 'own generation' and then 'fell asleep' (Acts 13:36). These believers are part of our spiritual family tree whose lives we should recall so that we might serve the Lord better in our own times.

Priests (12:1-26)

The first seven verses catalogue the twenty-two family names of **'the priests and Levites who returned'** ninety years earlier, in 537 B.C., from Babylon to Judah **'with Zerubbabel'** (12:1). A comparison with Nehemiah 10 shows that fifteen of the governor's contemporaries signed the covenant using these family names. How do we account for the fact that Nehemiah lists only twenty-two families, though twenty-four leaders were required for temple duties? (1 Chron. 24:1-18). Perhaps the priestly work was not fully operational at this stage.

The next two verses of Nehemiah (12:8-9) record the Levitical families at the time of the return from exile, whereas verses 10-21 tabulate the priests of the next generation. The fourth and final register (12:22-26) enumerates **'the family heads of the Levites in the days of Eliashib'** (22), the high priest when Nehemiah was governor of Judah (3:1,20,21; 13:28). It is clear from these lists that the priestly families did not change their names whenever a new leader was appointed.

Jeshua, or Joshua (12:10), was the son of Jozadak, also called Jehozadak, the high priest at the time of the exile (Ezra 3:2,8; 5:2; 10:18; Hag. 1:1; Zech. 6:11). The lineage of high priests from Aaron to Jozadak can be found in 1 Chronicles 6:3-15. The son of Jeshua, Joiakim, was high priest in the interval between Zerubbabel's return and the arrival of Nehemiah at Jerusalem in 445 B.C. There may have been other high priests during this time; if not, Joiakim's career lasted for almost a century. His son Eliashib was high priest during Nehemiah's term of office and one of Eliashib's grandsons was a son-in-law of Sanballat (13:28).

Zechariah (12:16) was the prophet and writer of the Old Testament prophecy who worked alongside Haggai to encourage the dejected temple builders (Ezra 5).

'The book of the annals' (12:23), translated as 'chronicles' in the Authorized Version, is not a reference to any biblical books but to temple archives relating to family records.

The identity of **'Jaddua'** (12:11) and **'Darius the Persian'** (12:22) has caused a great deal of scholarly debate,[1] and has an important bearing on the date of Nehemiah's oversight of Judah. Josephus, the Jewish historian, states that Jaddua lived many years later, at the time of Alexander the Great (356-323 B.C.), who conquered the Persian empire in 328 B.C. If this view is adopted it means that Nehemiah could not have known Jaddua unless he was governor at a much later period. But Nehemiah himself tells us that he was the Judean governor during the reign of King Artaxerxes I. There are several valid reasons for rejecting Josephus' identification of Jaddua. Firstly, he often gets his facts and dates wrong; furthermore, it was normal for Jewish parents to give their children the name of a father or grandfather. It is therefore possible that there was a Jaddua during Nehemiah's governorship and another priest of the same name in the days of Alexander, the Macedonian king. Further evidence for the reliability of Nehemiah's record is contained in fifth-century documents, known as the Elephantine Papyri, which identify the Darius mentioned in Nehemiah 12 as Darius II (423-404 B.C.), the sovereign who followed Nehemiah's patron Artaxerxes I. Darius II is called 'the Persian' to distinguish him from Darius I, 'the Mede', who threw Daniel into the lions' den (Dan. 6).

These registers of the priests and Levites reminded the Jews that the priesthood had deep roots in the past; therefore the priests were to be held in high esteem. We too should praise God for those who in the past brought us the gospel and ought to respect present spiritual teachers (Heb. 13:7,17).

Purity (12:30)

Nehemiah comes from poring over the dusty archives in the dimly lit chambers of the temple (12:1-26) to the joyful dedication of the walls of Jerusalem (12:27-43). The Levites, the singers and the musicians were invited to come into the capital city for the thanksgiving parade (12:27-29). But before the celebration could begin the priests and Levites had to purify themselves and their fellow Jews from ceremonial uncleanness (12:30). A similar requirement was demanded of the priests and Levites at the dedication of the temple in 515 B.C. (Ezra 6:20). The account of the purifying of the temple in the time of Hezekiah (Judah's thirteenth king who lived about 250 years prior to Nehemiah) gives us an insight into the thoroughness of such purification (2 Chron. 29). Animals were slain and their blood sprinkled on the sinful people and over the defiled utensils and furnishings. Then penitence gave way to praise! The elaborate ritual ablutions of the Old Testament were constantly driving home the message that God is holy and that his people are polluted with sin. Only those whose iniquities are washed away can worship or serve the Lord.

Praise (12:27-43)

At last the crushing hardship of years and the back-breaking labour of two months were replaced by the elation of a hard-fought victory and the exuberance of celebration as the singing Jews marched on top of the walls to the exhilarating sound of cymbals, harps, lyres and trumpets. This day, which was a memorable one for the nation and the culmination of Nehemiah's first term as governor of Judah, laid the foundation for future progress. Verse 27 resumes the historical narrative which was interrupted at 11:2.

The people were divided into two large choirs. Ezra led the first group (12:36) south towards the Dung Gate, past the Fountain Gate to the Water Gate. There is no mention of the Horse or East Gates; it is probable that they entered the city via the East Gate, which was close to the temple (12:31-37). The other choir moved away northwards in the direction of the

Tower of the Ovens, heading for the Jeshanah Gate, walking past the Fish Gate, the Towers of Hananel and the Hundred and the Sheep Gate to the Gate of the Guard (presumably the same as the Inspection Gate mentioned in 3:31), from which they entered Jerusalem (12:38-39). What memories must have flooded into the minds of the Jews as they walked the walls on which they had spent so much time and energy!

Nehemiah does not tell us the exact starting-point for the two choirs, but it seems likely that it was the Valley Gate. This would be an appropriate place to begin the choir procession because it was from this gate that Nehemiah set out on his nocturnal reconnaissance of the walls of Jerusalem (2:11-16). An astounding transformation had been achieved through the power of God in such a short time! The words **'to give thanks'** (12:31) translate one Hebrew word which means 'thanksgiving'; it is 'almost as though these choirs were the embodiment of what they sang'.[2]

The mass choirs converged, with a crescendo of praise, on the temple (12:40-42). This was a fitting place for the choirs to meet because the building of the walls was for the purpose of protecting the temple so that the Jews might worship their God in safety. Once in **'the house of God ... they offered great sacrifices, rejoicing because God had given them great joy'** (12:40,43). **'The women and children also rejoiced,'** and **'The sound of rejoicing ... could be heard far away'** (12:43). Verse 43 is in contrast to the time when the foundation of the temple was laid; then the joy of the people was mixed with the tears of the old men who remembered the splendour of Solomon's temple: 'No-one could distinguish the sound of the shouts of joy from the sound of weeping, because the people made so much noise. And the sound was heard far away' (Ezra 3:13). God can turn our weeping into joy! He has lost none of his power, nor has his love for his elect diminished over the years!

At the dedication of the city walls only the melody of joy

was heard: 'rejoicing ... great joy ... rejoiced ... the sound of rejoicing' (12:43). The source and focus of this joy was God himself: 'God had given them great joy.' This joy found its outlet in singing and the playing of music, though we ought to note that all the wall-builders sang, not just a few of them doing an 'item' at the front of the temple. We should also observe that the singing and the musical instruments were **'as prescribed by David the man of God'** (12:24,36). The same point is made about the giving of God's people in verse 44: **'the portions required by the Law for the priests and the Levites'**. To what extent are our worship and our stewardship regulated by the Word of God?

Provision (12:44-47)

Nehemiah turns the minds of his readers from the praise of God to the provision of food for the priests, Levites and the singers — even the gatekeepers were not forgotten. This final section of chapter 12 may seem like a bit of a comedown after the euphoria of the preceding verses. But what use is our worship of God, however enthusiastic, if it does not lead to practical godliness?

Nehemiah was a man to strike while the iron was hot; therefore **'at that time'** (12:44), which means either on that day or shortly afterwards, he put in hand arrangements to care for the needs of the spiritual leaders of the nation. In so doing Nehemiah was calling on the people to fulfil the promises made at the signing of the covenant (10:32-39). We read that **'Judah was pleased with the ministering priests and Levites'** (12:44). Sadly, this pleasure was short-lived (13:10). Cyril Barber makes an apposite comment: 'When we are right with God ... we will delight in those who minister to us in Christ's stead ... and count it an honour to see that they are properly supported in their work.'[3]

There is an interesting tie-up between praise and provision in Hebrews 13:15-16: 'Through Jesus, therefore, let us continually offer to God a sacrifice of praise — the fruit of lips that confess his name. And do not forget to do good and to share with others, for with such sacrifices God is pleased.' The balanced Christian does not separate sound doctrine from good deeds.

25.
'Remember me ... O my God'

Please read Nehemiah chapter 13

The year was 433 B.C. Nehemiah, the governor of Judah, packed his bags ready for the long, onerous journey back to the court of King Artaxerxes in Babylon. The events of twelve years flashed through his mind — the worship of God re-established and the capital city rebuilt and populated once again. Yes, all the hardship and labour had been worthwhile. If only Nehemiah had ended his book with chapter 12, or even at chapter 13:3, we should have a story with a happy ending! But happy endings belong to fairy stories; in the real world we constantly grapple with unfinished tasks, unsolved problems and unresolved conflicts. The Christian's life will have a happy ending — but not just yet!

Nehemiah was in for an awful shock when he returned some time later to Judah: idol-worshipping foreigners had married yet again into Jewish families; Tobiah, his arch-enemy, was resident in the temple; the Levites were pursuing secular employment through lack of financial support from God's people, and there was a Sabbath market in Jerusalem. The promises made in the sacred covenant (ch. 10) had been wilfully broken. Faithfulness to God declined while Nehemiah was away from the country. A lesser man than Nehemiah would have sunk into a black hole of depression, but he rolled up his sleeves and got stuck into his final reforms as governor of Judah. God had given him a work to do and he fulfilled that task regardless of setbacks and obstacles. The Lord who gave him strength in his previous spell as governor would empower him once more as he took up the reins again.

Where were Ezra the scribe and Hanani, Nehemiah's brother and the leader in Jerusalem, while the governor was away in Babylon? The fact that neither of these men is mentioned in Nehemiah 13 may suggest that they were now dead. If Hanani was still alive it may be that Eliashib, the priest, had manoeuvred him out of a position of leadership to effect his own wicked schemes. We can be sure that neither Hanani nor Ezra would have condoned the profane conduct of Eliashib or Tobiah; neither would they have tolerated this infringement of the Sabbath or the mixed marriages.

God's Word (13:1-3)

The time indicator, **'on that day'** (13:1), is imprecise in the Hebrew. It is evident from verses 6 and 7 that we are now in the period of Nehemiah's second term of office in Judah. We cannot be sure how long he was away in Persia, or the exact duration of this further stint of service, but we do know that he was no longer the administrator of Judah in 410 B.C. An Elephantine papyrus identifies the governor of Judah in that year as a man named Bagoas.[1] The important point to note about 'that day' is that **'The Book of Moses was read aloud in the hearing of the people'** (13:1). The reference to the Ammonite, Moabite and the mercenary prophet Balaam helps us to identify the passage read as Deuteronomy 23:3-6.

In Deuteronomy 23 God forbade acceptance of the Ammonites and Moabites, the descendants of Lot through incest with his daughters (Gen. 19:30-38) and the inveterate enemies of God's people. These two nations refused to provide food for

the nomad Jews in the wilderness. However, this prohibition
was not the expression of revenge or racial prejudice but a
spiritual safeguard for God's covenant race. The Moabites at
the time of Moses enticed the Jews into sexual immorality and
the worship of their idols with the result that 'the Lord's anger
burned against' his own people (see Num. 25). There was a
very real danger that the Moabites would have the same evil
sway on the Jews in the time of Nehemiah. In the long term the
separation of the Jewish race was a preparation for the coming
of Jesus Christ and the establishment of his kingdom. We too
are not to lower our standards of conduct so that we lose our
distinct identity as Christian people. The God who **'turned the
curse'** of Balaam **'into a blessing'** (Num. 22:1 - 24:25) for the
Jews will one day reward us in heaven (Matt. 5:11-12).

The reading of 'the Book of Moses' was not only public, it
was also powerful. It produced a change in the behaviour of the
hearers: **'When the people heard this law, they excluded
from Israel all who were of foreign descent'** (13:3). We
observe again that it was the communal reading of the law
which compelled the Jews to face up to God's demands for
them as his people (recall chs 8-9). The rest of Nehemiah 13
relates how God's people 'excluded from Israel all who were
of foreign descent'.

God's house (13:4-14)

If Nehemiah on his first arrival had been 'a whirlwind, on his
second he was all fire and earthquake to a city that had settled
down in his absence to a comfortable compromise with the
gentile world'.[2] The chief instigator of these concessions was
'Eliashib the priest' (13:4). Some commentators take the
view that Eliashib the priest mentioned here was not the same
person as Eliashib the high priest referred to in verse 28, whose

grandson was the son-in-law of Sanballat. It is argued that we would hardly expect the high priest to organize the contents of the storerooms.[3] However, we may assume that the high priest delegated much of this work to some of the other priests and Levites. Perhaps Tobiah was shown favouritism by Eliashib because he was related to the family of the high priest; we know for certain that he was connected by marriage to leading Jewish families and his Jewish name indicates that he was a nominal worshipper of Jehovah (6:17-18).

Eliashib and his fellow priests had done sterling work in rebuilding Jerusalem's Sheep Gate and the section of the wall which ran from the Tower of the Hundred to the Tower of Hananel, which was near the Fish Gate (3:1). But once Nehemiah left the city Eliashib's true character asserted itself when he provided the wicked Tobiah **'with a large room'** (13:5) in the temple for his personal use. This partiality towards Tobiah was reprehensible because he was an official of the banned race of the Ammonites (2:10,19), and because the room was required to store items used in the temple worship and the contributions given for the upkeep of the Levites and priests (13:4-5). Eliashib's policy was peace at any price, even if that entailed befriending those who hated God and were therefore the bitter enemies of Nehemiah. We may be sure that this sacrilege of the temple and conciliation with Tobiah upset the sincere worshippers of God who sup-ported Nehemiah, but they felt powerless to oppose the high priest. It is hard to speak up for God when opposed by the ecclesiastical hierarchy! It takes an unusual kind of courage to stand alone, like Athanasius, against the world.[4]

Kidner vividly captures something of the pleasure which this turn of events must have given to Tobiah: 'Tobiah never lacked audacity. Where even a toe-hold in the temple would have been a conquest, he obtains a room the size of a small ware-house, and has it cleared for him by the religious authorities themselves (7). It was doubtless a special satisfaction to see his personal belongings take precedence over the very frankincense for God and the tithes for His ministers; but the best of all he was at the nerve-centre of Jerusalem, ideally placed for influence and intrigue.'⁵

The provision of accommodation for Tobiah within the temple had far-reaching ramifications. Now there was no storage space for the produce given to the Levites and priests by the Jews; consequently their tithes gradually diminished. Moreover this meant that the Levites and other temple staff went back to their farms to scrape together a living (13:10). The words translated **'had gone back'** (13:10) in the Hebrew mean that the Levites had been forced to leave the city; the goodwill of chapter 12:44-47 had apparently vanished. The knock-on effect was a lowering of the spiritual temperature of God's people, seen in laxity of morals and the commercial enterprises which encroached on the Sabbath. It was at this period of Israel's history that the prophet Malachi appeared on the scene. It is evident from the book of Malachi that the nation was in a state of spiritual decline. He preached against the hypocrisy of the people and the wickedness of the priests (Mal. 1; 2). He accused the Jews of robbing God because they withheld their 'tithes and offerings' (Mal. 3:8-10). The prophet called for repentance and warned of judgement if his appeal was ignored (Mal. 3; 4).⁶

When Nehemiah returned to Judah he immediately did four things to rectify these abuses.

1. He turned Tobiah out of the temple (13:6-9)

Nehemiah personally threw Tobiah's belongings out of the temple and issued orders for the fumigation of the room. Then he changed it back into a storeroom for **'the equipment of the house of God, with the grain offerings and the incense'**

(13:9). He acted decisively because he believed that God's law must be obeyed whatever the cost. Church officers have no warrant to discipline members whose views differ from their own, but they must not evade their responsibility when there is a glaring disregard of God's Word in the life of the church. Problems which are not dealt with have a habit of growing into bigger problems later! Eliashib does nothing to oppose Nehemiah because he realizes that he cannot argue with God's Word. So in the church criticism is squashed when the leaders are seen to base their decisions on the guidelines laid down in the Bible.

2. He reproved the officials for their neglected duties (13:10-11)

Nehemiah was wise enough not to point the finger at the absentee **'Levites and singers'** (13:10), but rather to blame the officials for their remissness in fulfilling their duties (13:11). His question, **'Why is the house of God neglected?'**, recalled the broken promise of the officers when they signed the covenant: 'We will not neglect the house of our God' (10:39). However, 'The fine words were feeding nobody,' as Kidner aptly comments.[7] Nehemiah would not allow these leaders to nod in agreement and do nothing; he tells us that **'I called them together and stationed them at their posts'** (13:11).

3. He appointed trustworthy men for the distribution of supplies (13:12-13)

Eliashib was relieved of his obligations relating to the storerooms and this task was handed over to four reliable men appointed by Nehemiah: Shelemiah the priest, Zadok the scribe, Pedaiah a Levite and their assistant Hanan.

4. He asked God for favour (13:14)

Once again we are allowed to eavesdrop on the outpouring of
Nehemiah's soul to God. He addressed the Lord as **'my God'**
because he felt so much at ease in his relationship with God.
Three times in this final chapter of his memoirs he pleads with
God to remember him (13:14,22,31). This repeated plea was
a cry for God's help, apart from which Nehemiah's reforms
would have no lasting effect on the nation. In these prayers the
Judean governor sought the approval of God and also antici-
pated the reward which awaits all those who faithfully serve
the Lord. The Master's 'Well done!' was ample compensation
for the spiteful criticism and hurtful ridicule of Sanballat and
Tobiah. Nehemiah's delight in God expressed itself in his
concern for **'the house of my God and its services'**. The
temple was the place where God was present; therefore care
for the temple was an expression of his love for God. The
church is now God's temple (2 Cor. 6:16). We cannot love God
if we do not love his temple,the people of God (1 John 4:20-
21).

God's day (13:15-22)

Nehemiah's solicitude for the house of God was tied in with
his grief because of the desecration of the Sabbath, the day
designed for rest from labour so that time might be devoted to
the worship of God. When Nehemiah returned to Jerusalem he
saw some Jews treading winepresses on God's day, while
others were bringing merchandise into the city for the Sabbath-day market. The men of Tyre, residents of the capital city,
specialized in selling fish at this market (13:15-18).

It would seem that Nehemiah's use of the term **'loads'**
(15,19) was a conscious allusion to the words of Jeremiah. The

prophet stood at the gates of the city and declared God's message: 'This is what the Lord says: Be careful not to carry a load on the Sabbath day or bring it through the gates of Jerusalem. Do not bring a load out of your houses or do any work on the Sabbath, but keep the Sabbath day holy, as I commanded your forefathers. Yet they did not listen or pay attention; they were stiff-necked and would not listen or respond to discipline' (Jer. 17:21-23). God promised prosperity if his people obeyed his commands (Jer. 17:24-26), and punishment if they broke his laws (Jer. 17:27). God's threat was fulfilled when the armies of Nebuchadnezzar marched into Jerusalem in 586 B.C. and carried the Jews into seventy years of captivity. Nehemiah's reference to the Sabbath-breaking of their **'forefathers'** and the punishment which followed seems to confirm the idea that he had the passage from Jeremiah in his mind (13:17-18). Nehemiah's contemporaries were in danger of stirring up God's wrath again if they did not cease their Sabbath trading.

Nehemiah issued orders for the closure of the gates on the Sabbath and placed a guard to ensure that his instructions were carried out (13:19). Some of the merchants persisted in camping overnight outside the city so as to set up their wares early at the Sabbath market. Nehemiah's threats eventually convinced them that the mart was permanently closed! (13:20-21). Nehemiah gave the Levites a solemn charge to renew their devotion to God and **'to guard the gates in order to keep the Sabbath holy'** (13:22). The noise of buying and selling on God's day was a distraction to the temple worshippers and robbed the Sabbath of its true purpose of the adoration of God.

Christians are not bound by the elaborate and laborious regulations which governed the Jewish Sabbath. So what is the significance of this section to us today? The principle of one special day in seven for the cessation of labour and the corporate worship of God predates the Sabbath given to the

Jews at Sinai. The special day of worship has its roots in God's rest from work after the six days of creation and is laid down as a model for people of all ages and all cultures (Gen. 2:2). If the Sabbath was meant to be a delight to the Jews because they found their joy in the worship of God, how much more delightful should it be to us who rejoice in salvation through Christ? (Isa. 58:13-14).

Nehemiah's courageous reform of God's day was followed by earnest prayer to the God who was at the centre of that day (13:22). The appeal to God's pity and compassion, **'Show mercy to me'**, may suggest that Nehemiah's physical vigour was declining, so that he calls on the Almighty for strength. The words, **'great love'**, are from the same Hebrew word [*hesed*] that is translated as 'faithfully' in verse 14. This word is used about 250 times in the Old Testament and stresses loyal and faithful love. Nehemiah's steadfast and warm love for the Lord's people was patterned on, and a response to, God's tender love for him. Neither should we overlook the idea of divine generosity implied in the adjective 'great'.

God's people (13:23-29)

1. The people (13:23-27)

It is difficult for us in our tolerant age to appreciate Nehemiah's distress because of the marriage of Jewish men to foreign women. His reaction may seem to present-day readers bizarre and violent (13:25). However, various factors should be taken into consideration as we evaluate his drastic measures. We ought to bear in mind that Nehemiah was acting in his official capacity as the governor of Judah; his conduct was not merely that of a private individual. The inability to speak Hebrew by some of these children of cross-cultural marriages meant that they could not understand God's Word. Furthermore the foreign women came from infidel nations which worshipped idols. The distinct identity of the Jews as God's witnesses in the world was under threat (Isa. 43:9-12). They were repeating the sin of Solomon, Israel's third king, whose multiple marriages to ungodly women, in violation of God's law, brought suffering on the Jewish race for centuries (13:26-27; 1 Kings 11:1-13). The downfall of the wisest man warns us against the folly of spiritual declension. So in Nehemiah's time there was the danger that compromise could negate all the reforms that Ezra and Nehemiah had achieved in the past and have serious repercussions for the future. Will the church of tomorrow praise God for our faithfulness, or lament our failure?

Another difficulty in this concluding chapter of Nehemiah presents itself to us. Though Nehemiah reproved, pronounced God's curse, **'beat some of the men and pulled out their hair'**, and compelled them in God's name to take an oath not to repeat their past transgressions, he did not command them to leave their heathen wives (13:25). When Ezra dealt with the same evil his effective treatment was more radical and less explosive than that of Nehemiah, but it also unleashed many long-term heart-rending problems for the families involved in the divorces of Jewish men from their foreign wives and their children (Ezra 10). I think that Derek Kidner's comments help us to realize the dilemma confronting Nehemiah at this time: 'Ezra's major surgery was indeed highly efficient; but what of the flood of divorcees and uprooted children which it let loose on society? Any subsequent reformer would have had to choose between a repetition of this and the alternative of attempting less in the hope of achieving more. Which of these courses would constitute the lesser evil would have been far from evident.'[8]

2. The priests (13:28-29)

Nehemiah did not have one rule for the populace and another for those in positions of civil or religious authority. Personal compliance with, and the restraint of, those who offended God's law was always paramount for Nehemiah. The fairness of Nehemiah was in sharp contrast to the priests whom God 'humiliated before all the people' because of their 'partiality in matters of the law' (Mal. 2:9). The marriage of Sanballat's daughter into the high priest's family did not deter Nehemiah from expelling from the Jewish community **'one of the sons of Joiada'**, the Horonite's son-in-law and Eliashib's grandson. This forceful initiative was necessary for two reasons: firstly God's law laid down strict rules relating to the marriage of priests (Lev. 21:13-14); and secondly, the marriage of the priest to a daughter of Sanballat, the antagonist of Nehemiah, was a direct threat to the authority of the Judean governor. Nehemiah's forthright treatment of this apostate priest destroyed the pernicious influence of his enemies. Three times Nehemiah prays for God to remember him, now he beseeches God to remember to give Sanballat and his depraved allies the punishment which they deserved. This prayer is reminiscent of that in chapter 4:4-5 and recalls Nehemiah's sentiments in chapter 5:12-13.

Nehemiah's epitaph (13:30-31)

'I came, I saw, I conquered' was the boast of Julius Caesar — how different this is to the epitaph of Nehemiah: **'I purified ... [I] assigned ... I ... made provision...'** This epitaph reveals his humility and his devotion to the cause of God. These qualities, along with his godliness, courage and leadership abilities, come across repeatedly in this closing chapter, and indeed throughout the whole of his memoir. Right to the end he is concerned that each priest and each Levite should fulfil the task allotted to him and that wood should be provided for the temple so that God might be worshipped! Then he signs off with his last recorded prayer to God: **'Remember me with favour, O my God'** (13:31).

Chronological chart

539   Cyrus conquers the Babylonians.

538   Decree of Cyrus (Ezra 1:1-4).
A year later almost 50,000 Jews returned to Jerusalem under the leadership of Zerubbabel (Ezra 2).

536   Temple-building starts and halts (Ezra 3-4).

530-522   Reign of Cambyses.

522-486   Reign of Darius I.

520   Temple-building restarts after a break of sixteen years (Ezra 5).
Ministry of Haggai.

520-515   Ministry of Zechariah.

515   Temple completed (Ezra 6).
(The total number of years from beginning to end, including the break of sixteen years, was twenty-one years). The temple was finally rebuilt a little over seventy years after its destruction.

486-465   Reign of Xerxes I (Ahasuerus), husband of
            Esther.

486-480   Events of the book of Esther.

465-424   Reign of Artaxerxes.

458   Decree of Artaxerxes authorizing Ezra's return
            (Ezra 7:11-26).
            Ezra's arrival in Jerusalem, eighty years after the
            first return (Ezra 7-8).

450-425   Ministry of Malachi.

446   Decree of Artaxerxes suspending building of city
            (Ezra 4:17-22).

445   Arrival of Nehemiah in Jerusalem (Neh. 2).

445-433   Nehemiah serves as governor (Neh. 5:14).

444   The walls of Jerusalem were completed in fifty-
            two days (Neh. 6:15-16).

433   Nehemiah travels to Babylon.
            He later returned to Jerusalem for his second term
            as governor of Judah (Neh. 13:6-7).

410   'Nehemiah was no longer governor of Judah …
            for an Elephantine papyrus identifies the governor
            of Judah at that time as Bagoas.'[1]

References

Chapter 1 — Introducing Ezra
1. *The Bible in Outline* (various authors), Scripture Union (n.d), p.75.
2. *Ibid.*
3. Derek Kidner, *Ezra and Nehemiah (Tyndale Old Testament Commentaries)*, Inter Varsity Press, 1979, p.13.
4. There are two helpful Welwyn Commentaries on Haggai, Zechariah and Malachi: Michael Bentley, *Building for God's Glory* (Haggai/Zechariah), Evangelical Press, 1989; and John Benton, *Losing Touch with the Living God* (Malachi), Evangelical Press, 1985.

Chapter 2 — Home at last!
1. Josephus, *Antiquities of the Jews,* XI.5-6, cited by J. Carl Laney, *Ezra and Nehemiah (Everyman's Bible Commentary),* Moody Press, Chicago, 1982, p.22.
2. For information about Cyrus see F. Charles Fensham, *The New International Commentary on the Old Testament, The Books of Ezra and Nehemiah,* Eerdmans, 1982, pp.42-3.
3. Dave Cave, *Ezra & Nehemiah, Free to Build (Crossway Bible Guides),* Crossway Books, 1993, p.18.
4. Kidner, *Ezra and Nehemiah (Tyndale),* p.34.
5. Laney, *Ezra and Nehemiah (Everyman's),* p.24. Kidner discusses the identity of Sheshbazzar (*Ezra and Nehemiah (Tyndale),* pp.139-42). Compare Bentley, *Building for God's Glory,* p.25.

Chapter 3 — Only a list of names?
1. H. A. Ironside, *Notes on the Book of Ezra,* Bible Truth Depot (n.d.), pp.18-19.
2. There is an interesting note on the Urim and the Thummim in the Welwyn Commentary on 1 Samuel (Gordon Keddie, *Dawn of a Kingdom,* Evangelical Press, 1988, pp.228-9).
3. Kidner, *Ezra and Nehemiah (Tyndale),* p.43.
4. *Ibid.,* p.42.

Chapter 4 — Four essential ingredients for spiritual blessing
1. R. J. Tibbs, *Geneva Bible Notes,* May/June 1993, p.8.

Chapter 5 — An offer refused
1. Warren Wiersbe, *Why us?,* IVP, 1984, p.13.
2. Kidner, *Ezra and Nehemiah (Tyndale),* p.48.
3. Coleman Luck, *Ezra and Nehemiah,* Moody Press, 1961, p.37.

Chapter 6 — Coping with discouragement
1. Ironside, *Notes on the Book of Ezra,* p.57.
2. Kidner, *Ezra and Nehemiah (Tyndale),* p.53.
3. Cave, *Ezra & Nehemiah, Free to Build,* p.55.
4. J. G. McConville, *Ezra, Nehemiah, and Esther (The Daily Study Bible),* Saint Andrew Press, Edinburgh, 1985, p.35.

Chapter 7 — The temple completed
1. Kidner, *Ezra and Nehemiah (Tyndale),* p.57.
2. *Christian Hymns,* Evangelical Movement of Wales, 1977, no. 85.
3. Luck, *Ezra and Nehemiah,* p.43.
4. Cave, *Ezra & Nehemiah, Free to Build,* p.62.
5. McConville, *Ezra, Nehemiah and Esther,* p.39.
6. *Ibid.,* p.40.
7. Luck, *Ezra and Nehemiah,* p.48.

Chapter 8 — Ezra's self-portrait
1. Cave, *Ezra & Nehemiah, Free to Build,* p.71.
2. Kidner, *Ezra and Nehemiah (Tyndale),* p.62.
3. *Ibid.*
4. *The Bible in Outline,* p.75.
5. Kidner, *Ezra and Nehemiah (Tyndale),* p.63.

6. Laney, *Ezra and Nehemiah (Everyman's)*, p.54.
7. Kidner, *Ezra and Nehemiah (Tyndale)*, p.64.

Chapter 9 — The perilous journey
1. Cave, *Ezra & Nehemiah, Free to Build*, p.83.
2. Luck, *Ezra and Nehemiah*, p.58.
3. *Ibid.*, p.59.
4. Kidner, *Ezra and Nehemiah (Tyndale)*, p.65.
5. *Ibid.*, p.66.
6. P. Southwell, *Bible Study Commentary: Ezra-Job*, SU/CLC, 1982, p.13.

Chapter 10 — How to pray
1. Ironside, *Notes on the Book of Ezra*, p.85.
2. For more information about these nations and their geographical locations see Fensham, *The Books of Ezra and Nehemiah (NICOT)*, pp.124-5, and Cave, *Ezra & Nehemiah, Free to Build*, pp.96-7.
3. Kidner, *Ezra and Nehemiah (Tyndale)*, p.69.

Chapter 11— Holy people for a holy God
1. Letter (1990) to supporters from CARE — Christian Action Research & Education, 53 Romney Street, London SW1P 3RF.
2. Kidner (*Ezra and Nehemiah (Tyndale)*, pp.153-5) discusses the identity of Jehohanan, which has a bearing on whether Ezra came before Nehemiah or vice-versa.
3. Kidner, *Ezra and Nehemiah (Tyndale)*, p.70.
4. *Ibid.*
5. Luck, *Ezra and Nehemiah*, p.70.
6. Kidner, *Ezra and Nehemiah (Tyndale)*, p.71.
7. A. E. Cundell in the *New Bible Commentary: Revised 1970*, cited by Laney, *Ezra and Nehemiah (Everyman's)*, p.63.

Chapter 12 — Introducing Nehemiah
1. Kidner, *Ezra and Nehemiah (Tyndale)*, p.77.
2. Information in this paragraph has been culled from Cyril J. Barber, *Nehemiah and the dynamics of effective leadership*, B.McCall Barbour, Edinburgh. 1976, p.14.
3. *The Bible in Outline*, p.79.
4. *Ibid.*, p.81.

Chapter 13 — Sorrow and supplication

1. For an excellent summary of the life and work of Martin Luther read S. M. Houghton, *Sketches from Church History,* Banner of Truth, 1980, Section IV, pp.79-98.
2. Edward Donnelly, *The Evangelical Magazine of Wales,* Aug./ Sept. 1993.
3. *Ibid.*
4. Kidner, *Ezra and Nehemiah (Tyndale),* pp.78-9.
5. *Christian Hymns,* no. 346.
6. Barber, *Nehemiah and the dynamics of effective leadership,* p.21.
7. Laney, *Ezra and Nehemiah (Everyman's),* p.76.
8. Kidner, *Ezra and Nehemiah (Tyndale),* p.79.

Chapter 14 — Nehemiah's new job

1. Historical details relating to King Artaxerxes and Queen Damaspia can be found in Luck, *Ezra and Nehemiah,* p.88.
2. Kidner, *Ezra and Nehemiah (Tyndale),* p.80.
3. From the hymn by William Cowper, *Christian Hymns,* no. 399.
4. H. A. Ironside, *Notes on Nehemiah,* Bible Truth Depot, New York, 1913, p.16.
5. Kidner, *Ezra and Nehemiah (Tyndale),* p.81.
6. Information derived from Barber, *Nehemiah and the dynamics of effective leadership,* p.31.
7. Andrew Bonar, *Robert Murray M'Cheyne — Memoir and Remains,* Banner of Truth, 1966, p.23.
8. Kidner, *Ezra and Nehemiah (Tyndale),* p.82.
9. *Ibid.,* p.83.

Chapter 15 — Sharing the workload.

1. Luck, *Ezra and Nehemiah,* p.93.
2. Kidner, *Ezra and Nehemiah (Tyndale),* p.87.
3. Douglas Dawson, *Geneva Bible Notes,* July/August 1993.
4. McConville, *Ezra, Nehemiah and Esther,* p.89.
5. Barber, *Nehemiah and the dynamics of effective leadership,* p.51.
6. Kidner, *Ezra and Nehemiah (Tyndale),* p.87.

Chapter 16 — 'Our God will fight for us!'

1. Barber, *Nehemiah and the dynamics of effective leadership,* pp.59-60.

2. Kidner, *Ezra and Nehemiah (Tyndale)*, p.90.
3. In Genesis 16 we read of 'the angel of the Lord' visiting Hagar, the maid of Sarah, wife of Abraham. She identifies this angel as the Lord: 'She gave this name to the LORD who spoke to her: "You are the God who sees me," for she said, "I have now seen the One who sees me"' (Gen. 16:13; cf. Exod. 33:12-15).
4. Barber deals with the interpretation of the imprecatory passages of the Bible (*Nehemiah and the dynamics of effective leadership*, pp.62-4). A helpful book on this subject is James E. Adams, *War Psalms of the Prince of Peace*, Presbyterian and Reformed Publishing Company, New Jersey, 1991.
5. Barber, *Nehemiah and the dynamics of effective leadership*, p.65.
6. Kidner, *Ezra and Nehemiah (Tyndale)*, p.91.
7. The exact meaning of the latter part of verse 23 is difficult to determine. Derek Kidner comments briefly on the various translations of the Hebrew (*Ezra and Nehemiah (Tyndale)*, p.94).
8. *Christian Hymns*, no. 719.

Chapter 17 — Rich man, poor man
1. McConville, *Ezra, Nehemiah and Esther*, p.96.
2. Barber, *Nehemiah and the dynamics of effective leadership*, p.77.
3. *Kidner, Ezra and Nehemiah (Tyndale)*, p.95.
4. *Ibid.*
5. *Ibid.*, p.97.
6. Luck, *Ezra and Nehemiah*, p.104.
7. D. A. Carson, *A Call to Spiritual Reformation*, IVP, 1992, p.15.
8. Barber, *Nehemiah and the dynamics of effective leadership*, p.95.

Chapter 18 — Pressure and priorities

1. Kidner, *Ezra and Nehemiah (Tyndale)*, p.98.
2. Barber, *Nehemiah and the dynamics of effective leadership*, p.99.
3. Kidner, *Ezra and Nehemiah (Tyndale)*, p.99.
4. From a poem by a nineteenth-century American poet, Wallace William Ross.
5. Information drawn from Fensham, *The Books of Ezra and Nehemiah (NICOT)*, p.27.
6. Laney, *Ezra and Nehemiah (Everyman's)*, p.95.

Chapter 19 — The new community

1. Kidner discusses the problems relating to the translation of the Hebrew (*Ezra and Nehemiah (Tyndale)*, pp.102-3).
2. McConville, *Ezra, Nehemiah and Esther*, p.112.
3. Kidner, *Ezra and Nehemiah (Tyndale)*, p.102.
4. Luck, *Ezra and Nehemiah*, p.111.

Chapter 20 — 'The people of a book'

1. Kidner, *Ezra and Nehemiah (Tyndale)*, p.106.
2. *Ibid.*, p.104.
3. For a brief account of the life and hymns of Isaac Watts read Elsie Houghton, *Christian hymn-writers*, Evangelical Press of Wales, 1982, chs 10-11. A fuller life of Watts has been written by David Fountain: *Isaac Watts Remembered*, Gospel Standard Baptist Trust, 1974.
4. Thomas Watson, *All Things for Good*, Banner of Truth, 1992, p.8.
5. Ian Barclay, *Down with Heaven (Living out the fruit of the Spirit)*, Falcon Books, 1975, p.21.
6. Kidner, *Ezra and Nehemiah (Tyndale)*, p.109.
7. *Ibid.*

Chapter 21 — Amazing grace!

1. Laney, *Ezra and Nehemiah (Everyman's)*, p.104.
2. *Ibid.*, p.105.
3. Barber, *Nehemiah and the dynamics of effective leadership*, p.133.
4. The chronology of the events in the lives of Abraham and Moses is discussed in detail by Leon Wood, *A Survey of Israel's History*, Pickering and Inglis, London, 1970, pp.30-37,88-109.
5. McConville, *Ezra, Nehemiah and Esther*, p.126.

Chapter 22 — The covenanters

1. McConville, *Ezra, Nehemiah and Esther*, p.131.
2. Information derived from McConville, *Ezra, Nehemiah and Esther*, p.128, and checked with Robert Young's *Analytical Concordance to the Holy Bible*, Lutterworth Press, 1979.
3. Barber, *Nehemiah and the dynamics of effective leadership*, p.141, footnote.
4. Laney, *Ezra and Nehemiah (Everyman's)*, p.108.
5. *Ibid.*

Chapter 23 — Praise the Lord for volunteers!
1. Kidner, *Ezra and Nehemiah (Tyndale)*, p.117.
2. *Ibid.*, p.117.
3. There are twelve psalms which bear the name Asaph (50, 73-83). Asaph, David's musician, could not have written all of these psalms because several of them were composed after his death. It is clear from 2 Chronicles 29:30 that Asaph wrote some psalms, whereas others were written by David for the use of Asaph and the tabernacle choir (1 Chron. 16:7).
4. Kidner, *Ezra and Nehemiah (Tyndale)*, p.120.
5. For a map of the rural villages in Nehemiah's time and their present-day locations see Cave, *Ezra & Nehemiah, Free to Build*, pp.214-18.

Chapter 24 — Songs of praise
1. For further information on this debate consult Kidner, *Ezra and Nehemiah (Tyndale)*, pp.123-4 and Appendix III, pp.143-6.
2. *Ibid.*, p.126.
3. Barber, *Nehemiah and the dynamics of effective leadership*, pp.164-5.

Chapter 25 — 'Remember me ... O my God'
1. Laney, *Ezra and Nehemiah (Everyman's)*, p.128.
2. Kidner, *Ezra and Nehemiah (Tyndale)*, p.129.
3. Fensham says, 'He must be someone different, because it would be strange to mention that he was an overseer of the chambers if he was the high priest' *(The Books of Ezra and Nehemiah (NICOT)*, p.260). Dave Cave describes him as 'the equivalent of a dean' (*Ezra & Nehemiah, Free to Build*, p.240).
4. Athanasius was a third-century Bishop of Alexandria, in Egypt, who defended the deity of Christ against the unorthodox views of a man named Arius. He is remembered for his saying, 'Athanasius against the world,' meaning that if the whole world denied Christ's divinity he was prepared to defend it against all its opponents. A famous creed is named after Athanasius. For more information consult Tony Lane, *The Lion Book of Christian Thought*, Lion Publishing, 1984, pp.30-32.
5. Kidner, *Ezra and Nehemiah (Tyndale)*, p.129.
6. For further details on Malachi see Benton, *Losing Touch with the Living God*.

7. Kidner, *Ezra and Nehemiah (Tyndale)*, p.130.
8. *Ibid.*, p.153.

Chronological chart
1. Laney, *Ezra and Nehemiah (Everyman's)*, p.128.